HOW NOT TO MANAGE

A Quick Brown Fox Publications Book

First published in Great Britain by Quick Brown Fox Publications
in November 2008; this edition published by
Quick Brown Fox Publications in 2008.
Copyright © Kirkman/Mayhew 2008.

ISBN-10 0955480477 ISBN-13 9780955480478

Cover image © Chris Goodier, 2008. Used with permission.

Quick Brown Fox Publications is an independent publisher. They
want to hear from first time authors so please get in touch. They'd
love to hear from you. Please recommend this book to a friend
as they'd be very grateful.

www.quickbrownfoxpublications.co.uk

Please visit our *How Not To Manage* websites at:

www.slagoffyourboss.com
www.hownottomanage.com

HOW NOT TO MANAGE

Adam Kirkman
and
Daniel Mayhew

with
Chris Goodier

For Rob, Joff and Andy – DM

For Jojo, love GC

HOW NOT TO MANAGE   5

"The only management book you'll ever need...I've wondered for years why I was doing what I was doing, and this book explained it all...thank you, *HNTM*!"
– *Stuart Anderson, HR Manager, ACE Scaffolding Supplies*

"For years I was worried that I was being such a massive racist, but *How Not To Manage* showed me that I was just being normal!"
– *Thomas Smith, Assistant Manager (Part-time)*
Pizza Planet, Swindon

"The sheer lack of unimportance of this book in improving my vocabulary cannot be misunderestimated."
– *Pauline Costa, Finance Director,*
Doncaster Carpets and Floor-coverings

"I used to suffer delusions of grandeur, but not any more. This wonderful book has taught me to *enjoy* delusions of grandeur."
– *James Laing, Marine Life Manager,*
Pets At Home

"No, you can't have a quote for your book. How did you get in here? Get out of my office before I call security."
– *Lorraine Newcombe, Assistant Regional Manager,*
Taylors Dog Food

"Before reading this book I doubted that I had sufficient people skills to succeed in management. Now I know that I didn't need those skills in the first place."
– *Chris Hughes, Senior Supervisor, Wrexham Plastics*

Foreword by Rudy Sachs,
Professor of Progressive Management,
University of Delaware

When the authors contacted me to ask if I would write the foreword for this book, my first reaction was, "Who are you and how did you get this number?" However, after ten minutes or so, it became clear to me that we were very much speaking the same language. This was important because I can't speak German, Dutch or Italian, for example. Although the authors impressed me with their voices and words, what convinced me to contribute to this book was the cash they offered.

This powerful volume is a breakthrough in management literature. Of course, there are many other management manuals, but what sets this apart is its tailoring of the subject matter to the very managers who need it. Other management books include a bewildering array of techniques that the modern manager can employ. But these techniques invariably require a level of commitment and intellect that many managers simply do not possess. The importance of this point is illustrated by recent research which indicated that the average IQ of managers in the United Kingdom is 43.

The genius of *How Not To Manage* is that the techniques it describes require absolutely no effort, no intelligence, no interpersonal skills and no thought to implement. In this sense, this breakthrough text takes management manuals to a new level. This truly is Management 2.0.

Rudy Sachs,
Delaware, November 2008.

QUIZ:
What kind of person are you?

Answer the following questions as honestly as you can:

* ★ Do you strive for excellence in everything you do?
* ★ Do you expect the very best from yourself and others?
* ★ Do you have a very firm idea of where you will be in five years?
* ★ Are you short-tempered with people who don't measure up to your standards?
* ★ Are you very critical of yourself and others?
* ★ Do you spend a lot of time thinking about your work?
* ★ Do you find yourself being impatient with the ideas of others, just waiting to put forward your own ideas?
* ★ Do you get involved in office politics?

If you answered mostly 'yes' to these questions, then you sound like a bit of a dick.

However, on the upside, you are very well suited to management. You've brought the raw materials to this manager-manufacturing machine: reading this guide will take those raw materials and turn you into the World's Greatest Boss. Guaranteed.

ASK YOURSELF...

"AM I INSPIRED?"

ASK YOURSELF...

"AM I INSPIRING?"

STEP ONE:

HOW TO IMPROVE YOU

ASK YOURSELF... "AM I INSPIRED?"

If you're not inspired, how can you expect your staff to be? Sure, they have you to inspire them, but who do you have? You may have to do some serious soul-searching to fully answer this question. Perhaps you're not inspired. Maybe you're running on empty. Just going through the motions. Don't panic. This happens to everyone at some time. You just need to reconnect with the passion you once had for the job. Try slashing people's pay, or shouting at an errant employee. If you can dish your bad mood or hangover out onto someone else, you'll feel better, and your passion will return.

ASK YOURSELF.... "AM I INSPIRING?"

You have to inspire your workforce, both to work harder and more efficiently, but also to become better human beings. Remember that your employees view you as a god, and it's your duty to give them the best god ever. This all sounds pretty tough, but this first section gives you all the help and advice you need on How To Improve You. Now, we know the only acceptable management weakness is perfectionism. We understand that you're pretty much perfect. But we also think that, deep down, if you're really honest with yourself, maybe you know that you could use our help. Read on...

Listening is an important skill. As a manager, you will naturally spend most of your time talking, but occasionally you will have to listen to your employees talk. Most workplaces now operate an "open door" policy, where all employees are free to approach their manager to discuss any issues they feel are relevant to their job. As you can guess, this idea increases accountability and kills productivity.

Luckily, the resourceful manager has a coping strategy: multi-tasking. The successful manager should be able to multi-task with their time, so that while an employee is speaking to you, you are free to be able to work on other projects.

Remember that thought is four times faster than speech, so you should have no trouble increasing your productivity four-fold. Occasionally, this can result in an employee feeling that they do not have your full attention. You can, however, alleviate these worries by using a few simple tricks:

NODDING AT REGULAR INTERVALS. The noise of the employee speaking will create a kind of drone in your head. When the noise changes slightly in pitch, or there is a break in it, this is a good time to nod slightly, as if you were attracting a waiter, or passing a male colleague in the corridor. Nodding shows the employee that you are listening.

LOOKING AT THE SPEAKER. It is important not to let your head turn all over the place. The speaker must feel that they have your complete attention. If you are struggling to look at them for a long period of time, perhaps because of their intense ugliness, you can spend your time thinking which celebrity they would have to shack up with to produce a normal-looking child.

BE ATTENTIVE. At appropriate points in the conversation, you may also smile, frown, laugh, or be silent. Remember that you listen with your face as well as your ears!

A NOTE. One thing that is vital, however, is that you do not take notes. Notes are a form of weakness and indicate that you have a poor memory. As a manager, you should rely on other people to make notes, but it's preferable to ask someone to keep notes after a meeting or conversation. Asking them before can make them nervous, or mean they are too busy note-taking to contribute to the discussion.

How To Talk Authoritatively About Anything

Some management experts recommend that you model an approach where you admit to your limitations and openly tell people if you do not know anything about a given subject. They suggest actively seeking the knowledge of others and creating a learning environment where ideas and expertise are shared for the good of the team. These experts, however, are wrong. It is vitally important for the modern manager to be able to talk about anything at all and convince people that he or she is an expert. If this seems daunting, do not fear. Here's how to do it:

TALK LOUDLY. Everyone respects someone who talks really loudly all the time. In fact, scientists have proved that it doesn't actually matter what you say as long you say it loudly enough.

REFLECT BACK. This classic approach involves asking the person who has just asked you a question the exact same question back! It's so simple. Here's an example: Q - "Do you think the proposed merger would be beneficial?" A - "Do *you* think the proposed merger would be beneficial?"

LET SOMEONE ELSE SPEAK. While this might seem a strange approach at first, give it a try. If you are asked about something you have no knowledge of, simply say, "Well, I have got a lot to say on that particular issue, but before I do, I'd be interested to hear what Simon thinks about it."

POKER FACE. In order to achieve a successful poker face, you'll need to really, really concentrate on deciding what to have for lunch. Imagine yourself in the canteen, or in the sandwich shop. Try not to lick your lips. You'll have a far away look on your face that won't give anything away.

RUN THE NUMBERS. If you're pressed into a specific answer and you can't think quickly enough, tell them that you're going to have to "run the numbers on that one." Go back to your office, shut the door, and load up YouTube. Hopefully, whoever asked you the question will forget to come back. If they do, and press you further, you can just use the Magic Words. (See *How To Use The Magic Words.*)

Sometimes, the techniques in *How To Talk Authoritatively About Anything* are not enough and you may be on the verge of admitting to not knowing something. Don't give in! In an emergency, there is a sentence you can say that will instantly garner respect, lend you an air of gravitas and answer any question on any subject. And those glorious words? "I have always admired the stoicism of Nelson Mandela."

All good managers can use this technique. Here are a couple of examples:

You are in a team meeting and your staff are complaining about what they see as their systematic de-skilling in the New Labour audit culture which places unacceptable constraints on their professional autonomy. You are not really following it and don't know what they mean. Don't panic, just say, "I have always admired the stoicism of Nelson Mandela." That will shut them up.

Or you may be socialising with clients. One of them asks you if you agree that the War on Terror is a fiction created by the US neo-cons in order to secure support for illegal wars whose aim is to secure vital natural resources at the expense of others now and in the future. You don't know what this nutjob is talking about and you think he may be a Communist or something. But you need to impress him. Again, there is no need to panic. Just say, "I have always admired the stoicism of Nelson Mandela," and he will probably hug you.

The beauty of this phrase is that it always, always works. If you work for a soulless global organisation which exploits the people or resources of the third world out of pure greed, it doesn't matter. If you live a vacuous existence of conspicuous consumption, it doesn't matter. If you have nothing in your life apart from your desire to exercise power over others to make up for the fact you wet the bed until you were ten, it doesn't matter. And it doesn't matter because you just said 'Nelson Mandela.'

How To Give A Presentation

Many managers find public speaking to be an area in which they experience difficulty. While this is a normal response for many, it need not be for you. A modern manager like you will not fear public speaking, but rather see it as a great opportunity to experience one of the most satisfying and glorious phenomena on God's earth – the sound of your own voice. Here are some tips:

ACT NATURALLY. Whilst acting naturally is appropriate in some contexts, such as when you are asleep or paralyzed with grief, it is not the way to act in the workplace and is certainly no way to give a presentation. Remember that your audience will not be impressed with a speaker who merely tells them what they need to know. Be sure to talk really, really loudly and make exaggerated movements with your arms and hands. Glare at individual members of your audience or point at them aggressively to get their attention. As it is very likely that your staff are not as intelligent as you, be sure to repeat your points many times to ensure they understand. Experts stress the importance of eye contact. Be sure to lock eyes with every member of the audience for about thirty seconds at some time during your presentation. Some staff may be resistant to holding your eye for this long. If this happens, do not panic. Simply stop the presentation until you have achieved the necessary length of eye contact. You may need to say "We can wait here all day."

USE VISUALS. Trained professionals have produced a huge amount of very useful data on the interaction of visual, kinesthetic and aural elements of presentations. This research, however, is really quite complicated and full of long words. All you need to know is this: every successful presentation ever made shares one feature – Microsoft PowerPoint. This fantastic piece of software enables you to project all your main points, or in fact every word you say, on to a big screen. Try to use every one of the transitions they offer. Remember that whilst sometimes 'less is more,' with PowerPoint, 'more is more.' Use as many slides as you can and be sure to add lots of clip art. Don't worry if it's not strictly relevant – stick it in anyway! Your audience will thank you for it.

TIMING. Correctly judging how long your presentation should last is vital. Most experts agree that thirty minutes is the optimum duration for a presentation. You should therefore aim to double this, as this will make your presentation twice as good.

BE AWARE OF CULTURAL DIFFERENCES. In today's multinational business world, you may be given a presentation by someone from another country. You may notice some differences in style depending on the nationality of the speaker, for example, Americans will move around the room a lot and involve the audience. The British are more likely to stand still. The Swedes will have amazing cheekbones. The French will try to get off with the audience or start collaborating with the Nazis. Do not be afraid of these foreigners: they're still people. If their English is weak, talk even louder than before.

How To Communicate
Effectively With Others

One of the most important skills in your smart, executive arsenal is your ability to communicate with others. Government tests (involving a hilarious combination of blind and deaf subjects) have revealed that over 80% of communication is non-verbal. The remaining twenty percent is verbal communication, and it's this twenty percent that tests have proved is sixty percent more important than non-verbal communication. Already, this seemingly simple area has proved to be a real minefield for the modern executive. Luckily, everyone you will ever talk to at work can be split into three groups, and we give you some pointers on how to deal with them:

YOUR INFERIORS. These are people that you are in charge of, or who earn less than you. We're pretty sure that most people fit into this group. If you're not sure, try judging them on their appearance. It's quite easy to communicate with your inferiors, despite their inevitable stupidity. You'll need to speak louder and slower, of course, and it might help to repeatedly ask them if they understand. Feel free to patronise. Try using rhetorical questions, just to see if they're dumb enough to answer.

YOUR EQUALS. There are few people in the management world who are your equal. (There are few people in the world who are your equal, period.) They enjoy similar pay packets and power levels, and are roughly equal in terms of their age and good looks. They have similar desires, similar management styles, and similar jokes. These people are easy to communicate with as they are so similar to you. Be aware, though, that these are the kind of people that you need to destroy in order to get ahead. Try slagging them off behind their back, or ousting them in a management coup.

YOUR SUPERIORS. These rare people are the most wonderful people on earth. Upper management is the goal of every single human being on the planet, and these people have achieved it. They're like rock gods, football megastars and movie idols all rolled into one, and you must treat them as such. Bow to their superiority at all times. They hold the power to make or break your career, and hence your entire reason for existing on their planet. Your language must be obsequious and your body language grovelling.

How To Run A Conference Call

As such a successful manager, you will sometimes be required to co-ordinate large projects involving many different people across the country, or even the globe. Unfortunately, gone are the days of week-long business trips to the Bahamas to 'liaise' with a client. On the up side, the days of meeting in a Happy Chef off the M1 near Long Buckby are behind us. This has all been possible thanks to conference calls – nature's answer to carbon footprints.

However, all technology is slightly scary, and conference calls can be a minefield of miscommunication and bruised egos. Why not follow these simple rules for running a conference call?

HAVE AN AGENDA. The key to any successful meeting is to have an agenda, and this is no different with a conference call. But don't just have an agenda. Have a *hidden* agenda. Your hidden agenda should be to talk up your own achievements. Perhaps you should try belittling the other callers?

REMEMBER, YOU'RE UNSEEN. A fantastic facet of the conference call is that you cannot be seen. It therefore presents an excellent opportunity to catch up on other work, go for a walk or sleep. Anyone who has yawned, rolled their eyes or made wanker signs at people in a face-to-face meeting will know that this can create a level of awkwardness. But with conference calls, you can avoid this!

TAKE CARE OF HOUSEKEEPING. If the conference call is a regular one, and all conference calls should be, ensure that everyone is up-to-date with what happened on the last call. This should involve a detailed sentence-by-sentence recap. Feel free to 'do' other people's voices. If there is someone new on the call, ask them to introduce themselves to the rest of the team. Treat this like an interview so ask lots of personal questions. Teams work well when there is an understanding of trust built from this kind of knowledge. Also, make sure you lay out the ground rules at the very start. Insist that only one person speak at a time, and that that person be you.

BONUS POINTS. Award yourself one super special bonus management point for every time you can say "What?", "I can't hear you", "Can you repeat that please?" and "Can you hear me? Can you hear me now? How about now?" If you score over thirty, hang up and take the rest of the day off.

How To Avoid Giving Direct Answers

A direct answer is like a death sentence to a manager. It must be avoided at all costs – if you give a definite answer, and then things don't work out as you've dictated, you are left with very little room for manoeuvre. Even if you think you're fairly sure of the answer, don't risk it. Try one of these useful hints and tips instead:

USE STOCK PHRASES. Conventional wisdom tells us that it is better to be thought an idiot than to open your mouth and remove all doubt. What this really means is that the more you have to say, the smarter you are. Don't let silence be an option for you. Try and deflect the question by saying something like:
  ★ "Let's birdtable this discussion later."
  ★ "Can we touch base about that offline?"
  ★ "Don't you worry about Blank. Let me worry about Blank."

"CONFUCIUS SAY..." There was this Chinese chap called Confucius who lived to be about a thousand or something  so he was pretty wise. He had something smart to say about pretty much everything. If you're ever in trouble, just put on a slight Chinese accent (it may help to pull the corners of your eyes back a little) and say "Confucius say" and follow that with one of these:

* "If you think in terms of a year, plant a seed; if in terms of ten years, plant trees; if in terms of a hundred years, teach the people."
* "Our greatest glory is not in never falling, but in getting up every time we do."
* "Better a diamond with a flaw than a pebble without."

Be sure to follow these comments with a sage nod. If your colleagues seem unhappy with your Chinese accent, just say "Me velly solly" and bow slightly. Should they maintain a blank look, tap the side of your head and say "think about it" or "it's a grower" as you exit the room.

GET OUT OF JAIL FREE. Obviously, you must avoid being pinned down to a definite answer in case it turns out that something is your fault. Now, you may have made a mistake in the past and not been quick enough to distance yourself from it. Someone may in fact question why you made such a stupid decision. It's too late to avoid giving a direct answer; you should have done that months ago! Luckily, there's a get out of jail free card available on this one. You can redeem yourself with a simple "That's not how I remember it." Whoever's questioning you won't be able to call you a liar, but if they do, you can snarl aggressively at them "are you calling me a liar?"

How To Lie Plausibly

Theoretically, we know that lying is bad, but there is no way you can answer every question honestly. Questions such as "does my bum look big in this?" or "was it good for you too?" are simply invitations to lie in order to spare someone's feelings. In exactly the same way, you will need to lie in the workplace, too. In fact, a carefully-chosen and well-timed lie can make several people's lives better, and as long as at least one of those people is you, then you're doing the right thing. Here's how to lie, and lie well.

BE KNOWN FOR HONESTY. Carefully build up a reputation for honesty, or at least not dishonesty, by being brutal with people's tea-making skills, or perhaps by owning up to letting one go in the lift. People will believe that you are honest, which allows you to get away with really big lies, like you really were sick on the Friday before a Bank Holiday weekend, or that it really was Lorraine who stole from petty cash.

A similar trick is to become known as a really bad liar – telling people that you aren't scared of spiders, for instance, then freaking out when you see one. People will think you are a terrible liar and won't suspect a thing when you are lying to them.

TELL PEOPLE WHAT THEY WANT TO HEAR. People are more likely to believe a lie if it's what they want to hear anyway. This is particularly useful when dealing with your own boss, e.g. "Everything is on track with the current project. Your tie looks nice."

WIN THAT OSCAR! It's important that you act casual when lying. Try for an honest tone, make plenty of eye contact (but not too much) and make the lie plausible. To make sure it's plausible, ask yourself if you would believe your own lie. In fact, it's preferable if you do believe your own lie, because then, technically, you're not even lying.

"THAT ALL DEPENDS ON WHAT THE MEANING OF 'IS' IS." A technique straight out of Bill Clinton's book, this wonderful little gem involves using language to hide the truth. You can omit certain truths, imply something other than the truth, exaggerate, or even hide in a murky forest of euphemism. The genius of this technique is that you are simply being coy, while the person you're 'lying' to is technically jumping to conclusions, or even spreading malicious rumours themselves. Should you ever be caught in a lie like this, kick up a big fuss about this person's rumour-spreading or conclusion-jumping. If you make a big enough deal over it, you can make people forget your initial untruth.

How To Steal From Work

So, you want to steal from work? You're not alone. Every minute, over £2billion is wiped from the economy by employee theft. However, one employee in five will be dismissed for theft at some point in their career. Obviously, you're already stealing time from work. But although time is good, it doesn't help you furnish your house, or put food on the table. Companies expect, perhaps even demand, employees to take little items like pens, staplers and fridges, which are small fry for the office thief. This section details how you can gain the kind of bonuses that your own boss is denying you.

THE BASICS. Pick items that won't be noticed right away – it's not advisable to walk away with a colleague's monitor, for example. If you're not sure if the particular item will be missed, try moving it first to see if anyone notices. If no-one does within four working days, then feel free to take it home on the fifth.

WORK UNDERCOVER. Prime times to steal from work are when a colleague is leaving (be it for another job, retirement, or dismissal) or when new employees are starting. If anything is noticed to be missing, the blame will naturally fall upon the new employee, or on the recent leaver.

STEAL FOR THE THRILL. It's vital that you never let yourself be the prime suspect – for example, never steal anything that

you have previously expressed a great deal of admiration for, such as one of the new ergonomic chairs in Marketing or the electronic photo frame on your secretary's desk. You will instantly be a suspect. Instead, steal not for what you're stealing, but instead for the thrill of stealing. Like speeding, nicotine or spousal abuse, it's a rush. You may not even want what you're taking: this isn't a problem, there's always a car boot sale on somewhere nearby, or you can register for an eBay account under a pseudonym.

GET CREATIVE. Steal software from work, or RAM, or swap out hard drives for smaller ones. Take printer cartridges, too. If you work in a hotel, build up a lifetime's supply of toiletries. Working in a restaurant or bar gives you limitless options for feasting and drinking. Remember, in any customer-facing work environment, lost property is effectively just a box with 'FREE STUFF' written on the side.

DUST. Finally, if anything has enough dust on it, you can probably take it without anyone noticing.

Salaries are a sensitive issue in the workplace. How much do other people earn? Do they earn more than you? Luckily, there's always one rule with your salary: you're never earning enough. And it's always the right time to ask for more. There's no 'proper' way to ask for a salary increase – you can drop hints in earshot of your boss, or work very hard, but we've found that best of all is to speak to them directly, perhaps in a slightly confrontational manner. Here's how to get what you deserve:

JUSTIFY YOUR ACHIEVEMENTS. You need to be prepared when you enter into salary negotiations. You need to bring both anecdotal and quantifiable evidence. For anecdotal evidence, why not tell some tales of how you've kept workers downtrodden and malleable? Bringing quantifiable evidence of your successes is a real winner – for example, mention how you've slashed budgets, kept salaries low, and driven out the established, expensive employees.

KNOW YOUR WORTH. Do some market research to see what other people in similar positions at different companies are earning. Then you'll have an idea about what kind of figure you can ask for. Alternatively, you can calculate the perfect pay raise by using a secretive branch of microeconomics which dictates that there's a very precise perfect number for everything. This secretive economic theory dictates that if you drive at 78.5mph you can't have an accident – just try! Similarly, if you ask for a 63.4% pay raise, you can't be turned down.

EVIDENCE YOUR LONG-TERM GOALS. You have to show that you're worth investing in. Focus on developing your value to your boss within the marketplace by assuming many new responsibilities. What this means is promising to do loads of stuff, like reorganising the department, creating an efficiency drive or centralising customer integrity. The key word here is 'promise.' Once you've secured the salary, you don't actually need to do any of these things. And if they don't give you a raise, then you definitely don't need to do any of these things.

USE BLACKMAIL. Lastly, of course, if you're unsuccessful using all the other techniques, resort to blackmail. If you don't have anything on them, make it up and then go over their head.

Management is stressful. New York will be breathing down your neck in six hours; Beijing has already been hard at work for ten. To compete at the highest level, you have to burn the midnight oil at both ends. You're trying to manage a team of buffoons and the restraints of a conventional office system have shackled your creativity and the weight of responsibility has crushed your resourcefulness. There's no two ways about it: you're under a great deal of stress, which the government has decreed is bad for you. Luckily, we have some tips to help you deal with stress:

SHOUT AT SOMEONE. This always relieves stress. Either pick an employee that you hate – perhaps they once made a sarcastic comment towards you – or you can simply settle for the first person you see and berate them. Remember, you don't need a reason or excuse. Just go for it. Try to keep your tirade focused on their ability to perform their job, but if you stray into personal territories it doesn't matter that much. If you can make them cry then you'll definitely feel better about yourself.

THROW MONEY AT THE PROBLEM. Why not give yourself a pay raise? This often makes the stresses and strains easier to manage. You may find it hard to give yourself a pay raise, but you can always disguise it as a management bonus. Alternatively, you may want to reward yourself with more holiday. It's your decision, although if you're too stressed out to think straight, just flip a coin.

DRINK HEAVILY. Another wonderful way to deal with stress is to binge drink. Studies show that alcohol helps you forget your problems. You may also want to consider overeating. Psychologists will tell you that it's not healthy to bury your feelings in food and drink: but they also think that stuff that happened in your childhood affects you now. Idiots.

GET SIGNED OFF. The long-term effect of stress is to cause stress-related illness, and stress-related illnesses account for over eighty percent of management sickness. Symptoms include lethargy, depression and insomnia. Most doctors will sign you off just to get rid of you – why not cry a little bit in the waiting room? They'll give you a sick note just to get rid of your clever representation of a tearful loser.

RELIEVE THE TENSION. Many executives like to use little rubber stress balls which they can squeeze and assault violently in order to relieve the stress. Why not try this with your secretary, or spouse? Or, if you're so inclined, perhaps even with your own balls? Have you seen *There's Something About Mary*? Why not lock yourself in your office, pull the blinds, and take the matter into your own hands. In five minutes or so you'll be feeling more relaxed.

Today's modern manager will often be leading the team bonding sessions in the local boozer (see *How To Bond With The Lads: For Men*) and it has been found that this can negatively affect the body the following day. You may also  be under a great deal of stress, and one of the utterly unavoidable side-effects of stress is alcoholism. (See *How To Deal With Stress*.) Either way, it is important that you continue to manage at peak efficiency, even if you don't feel great. Here are some tips about how to manage with a hangover:

COME IN LATE. After all, you were up quite late last night, and you'd probably only be stuck in traffic if you tried to make it in on time. You're probably feeling tired and a little poorly so stay in bed for a while. Besides, the rules of time-keeping don't apply to you because you are better than the rest of your workforce. This also applies to going home early, or taking a long lunch.

MANAGE BY E-MAIL. True managerial excellence can be achieved without face-to-face or voice contact. Just set out the tasks you want your staff to achieve. Make the important ones bold so they know what to focus upon. There should be no reason for people to speak to you, especially loudly.

BRAG ABOUT HOW MUCH YOU DRANK. Research indicates that the amount of alcohol you consume is directly proportional to how sexually attractive you are. It stands to reason that talking about how much you drank last night – preferably exhaustively listing what you drank and in which establishment – will also make you sexually attractive to your listeners.

POWERNAP. Arrange your office so you can take mid-morning and mid-afternoon powernaps. The mind, with its delicate balance of ego, id, and superego, allows the most intense thought just before you fall asleep as the conscious mind relaxes enough to allow the subconscious mind through – which is why you always remember vital pieces of information just before you fall asleep at night. A good manager will enforce blanket measures to ensure these vital pieces of information do not remain undiscovered until last thing at night by powernapping during the day.

START DRINKING AGAIN. Being a good manager is a little bit like being drunk. Being loud and repetitive are good places to start. Like the authority of a management position, alcohol enables you to make sexual advances on all and sundry.

There will come a point in your management career when you suddenly realise that a large portion of your life has been wasted. You have given hour after hour of your life in endless, thankless service, until the years have piled up to drain you of all happiness. Eventually, you realise that you care more about work than your family. They have been holding back your career and you resent them for it. There's a certain stigma attached to placing career before family: but all pioneers are ridiculed. They laughed at Columbus when he said he'd sail to the moon. But you're right, as always. Here are a few tips on how to handle the awkward conversations:

PARENTS. It's a relief to tell your parents that you'd rather be at work than with them. By the time you've realised that work's the most important thing to you, your parents will be getting on in years, and you'll have realised that they won't be around forever. You might as well prepare for the inevitable and begin to cut them out of your life now. Stop returning their calls and cancel all engagements with them at the last possible moment, and avoid rescheduling. If they're a bit senile, you can pretend you're going through a tunnel when they call, even when they ring your home number.

SPOUSE. Living a lie can be a horrible thing. You've promised to love and cherish someone *forsaking all others*, possibly for real in a wedding or just for a laugh to shag them, and then all of a sudden you find yourself trapped in a dangerous love triangle. You have to be honest with your spouse and tell them, straight up, that they're not as important to you as your job is. Explain to them that you would be able to achieve everything you wanted if only you had the freedom to work late, or at weekends. Perhaps you can emphasize to them that it's their fault you aren't in senior management yet. You can even be as honest as to tell them that you're usually thinking of the job while you're "on the job," and that you even sneaked away to work on your honeymoon.

CHILDREN. Telling a child that they're not as important to you as your job is probably one of the hardest things you'll ever have to do. It's probably best that you never tell them. Instead, why not try ignoring them when they try and talk to you, or shouting at them if they play noisily? If you have teenagers, they probably won't want to talk to you anyway, so that'll be fine. One of the major benefits in not caring about your children anymore is that you no longer need to sit through awful school plays, or freeze through low-quality football matches, or pay for stupid piano lessons. In fact, dumping your family is a great way to maximise your personal profits.

TIMING. Timing is everything when breaking up an otherwise happy family. Why not choose Christmas? There's always tons of food and lots of stuff on TV to cheer up your broken-hearted family, and the office is usually fairly empty, so you can just crack on with work.

The law of averages indicates that eventually your company will hire someone that you consider to be sexually attractive and not just 'office pretty.' Not that there's anything wrong with 'office pretty.' (See also: *How to Interview*.) You may also find that they are interesting to talk to as well, and as a result you may consider initiating a romance upon them. Or, you may just want to work your way through the office. All workplace romances should come with a warning, especially as a manager: they are absolutely fraught with delightful possibilities. Here are a few tips:

FLIRTING. Let them know you are interested by flirting with them. Laugh at their jokes, listen to their stories. Be sure to flirt openly and quite lecherously with the employee, especially in front of their friends. This indicates that you are interested. Remember, it's more important to appear interested than to appear interesting.

BE INTERESTED IN WHAT THEY SAY, NOT JUST HOW THEY LOOK. This is the golden rule of initiating an office romance. Both men and women appreciate it when you take an interest in their opinion, especially before you have told them what their opinion is.

MARK YOUR TERRITORY. You may not be the only person who has noticed the allure of this particular employee. Should you notice someone else making their moves upon them, do whatever is necessary to remove them from the picture. Reorganise the department. Rotate the seating arrangement. Spread rumours they're a gay.

FAVOURITISM. It is more than acceptable to treat one employee more favourably than another, especially if you fancy them. Be sure to pick them for tasks that involve you working closely together, and apportion the workload so that the two of you have plenty of free time. Excuse them from late meetings or difficult tasks, and always offer to shift their workload to other, less attractive colleagues.

SEAL THE DEAL. Office parties are a great place to make a clumsy move upon your intended. Why not throw a party for a spurious reason, like celebrating Elton John's birthday? It's important that both of you are liquored up – your prospective partner even more so than you. Feel free to add shots to their drinks to add to the party atmosphere (vodka is a good bet as it's odourless.) If the party is taking place in the office, remember that using the photocopier isn't just a cliché, it's mandatory. Also, remember that photocopier glass isn't as strong as you think.

Should the worst happen, and they either reject your advances or your romance ends under disharmonious circumstances, then you can always transfer them to another branch or fire them for gross misconduct. They were probably a gay anyway.

Your customers are not unlike your staff. Both groups are pigs and deserve nothing more than your contempt. And what better way to express your contempt than through advertising! Here's how:

PRETEND YOU GIVE A SHIT. If you work for a brewery, entreat your customers to 'drink responsibly.' Like you care! You may laugh but it really works. If you want to advertise your chain of supermarkets, pretend that you are 'committed' to lowering prices because you want to lower the cost of living for families across the land. Make it sound like social work. Customers love this shit! Sit back and watch the chump change roll in.

YOUR CUSTOMERS DO NOT WANT YOUR PRODUCT, THEY WANT A BETTER LIFE. Remember, never try to sell your product on its benefits. Instead, you must sell your customers the life they really want. If you are advertising a car aimed at middle-aged married couples, have a TV advert featuring a middle-aged married couple that still shag! Or, if your company sells games consoles for fat children who never go outside, pretend that using it is good exercise!

PRETEND YOU ARE MAKING THE WORLD A BETTER PLACE. Don't sell your mobile phone network by telling people it's cheap or reliable. Instead, tell them you are committed to 'connecting people' or 'bringing people together!' Commission an advert with lots of smiling people and a plinky-plonky 'homemade' soundtrack. Priceless.

At the moment, your pig-faced muppet customers are probably obsessed with the environment and so it will definitely pay off to pretend your product does something to help the end-zone layer.

Why not promise to donate money to some charity for every product they buy? While some of your profits will have to go to some do-gooding charity losers who have probably never even sat in a BMW, don't worry as you will have more profits than you would have done otherwise. It's the classic speculate to accumulate. While it seems ridiculous that consumers will actually swallow this garbage, trust us – they will!

Be aware that some companies have used this scam and gone a bit too far. Executives at Dove soap came up with a brilliant wheeze one night in the pub – a 'campaign for real beauty' to get ugly women to buy their products. Once they'd stopped laughing, they instructed their ad agency to come up with a series of adverts on this theme. Unfortunately, some of their staff didn't fully grasp the joke and stepped up the campaign without management's knowledge. This resulted in some right mingers getting on TV, and people are still chucking their guts up.

How To Research Management Techniques

There are literally hundreds of management guides on the market, each with their own buzzwords which latch onto fickle-minded managers and brainwash them into spouting gibberish. As a good manager, you should be aware of these texts and the ideas that they represent, but don't lose sight of the fact that your own ideas are usually better.

Now these books can be quite long and sometimes use big words, which we've already seen can be hard to understand. Here's a shortcut to making it look like you've read some of the top books on the market.

UNIFYING THEORIES. Most of the popular management guides decide that there is one Unifying Theory to describe how the world functions, a simple metaphor which explains everything from why milk usually smells sour through to why the Nazis were so popular. They tend to use their own special buzzwords – which you will need to incorporate into your own managementese to imply you have read the texts – and prove their theories with a few half-assed anecdotes about graffiti in New York or that swimming pool of gold from *Duck Tales*. Most guides reference experiments from around the world which lend their findings a degree of gravitas, perhaps in an attempt to indicate that the majority of their research wasn't just using Google and Wikipedia.

SPECIFIC BUZZWORDS. To appear like you have read these guides, it's important that you drop the following into regular conversation:

The Nudge: Use this to refer to a reminder that you might be on the verge of doing something you later regret – a little moment of clarity, like walking in on yourself watching porn.
Homers: This refers to people who make clumsy and obvious errors, but always in predictable ways. This refers to the fictional animated character Homer Simpson, star of *The Simpsons*, and not from the belief that the gays inevitably make mistakes as they are lesser-brained.
Thin Slicing: This term refers to making vastly important decisions based on limited research and knowledge. If you're happy to mix your metaphors, you can also use this in conjunction with 'the thin end of the wedge' to

incorporate the idea that you are somehow using your limited knowledge as a ramp to success.

ANECDOTES. Sometimes, buzzwords aren't enough to motivate people. They're still staring at you like slack-jawed yokels, begging for your wisdom. Luckily, a few simple stories can prove the unshakeable truth of pretty much anything, and here are a few tenuous examples for you to reference:

Fake Flies. In order to improve hygiene in men's toilets, a Dutch nightclub painted little flies on the back of the urinal, the theory being that men would try to hit this target. Astonishingly, cleanliness increased sixty-two fold almost overnight. The moral here: small things can make a big difference. Use this to explain why you're being anal about office supplies, or why you insist upon petty rules being followed inflexibly.

Because. People will do almost anything for you if you add the word 'because' into a sentence. The classic example is skipping a queue for the photocopier – people will let you ahead of them, even if your excuse is 'because I don't want to wait.' The moral here is that it's better to give a reason for your behaviour, rather than assuming the other party knows your reason. Use this to skip photocopier queues.

Buying BMWs. A friend of a friend of a friend who vowed never to buy a BMW because "everyone else already has one" decided to buy one anyway, but only after test-driving other cars. The moral of this story is that you make up your own reasons for changing your mind. Use this anecdote to show off that you own a BMW, but that it doesn't make you the same as all your other management pals who own BMWs.

The phrase 'think outside the box' is, without doubt, mankind's greatest and most important achievement. This beautiful sentence rings through boardrooms and offices up and down the land, and rightly so. The miracle that is modern Britain was built on this phrase. You should ensure that you implore your staff to think outside the box at least fourteen times a day. We are sure you already do. As you no doubt know, your employees will be inspired and grateful every time you use this magnificent phrase. Many managers have mastered the skill of saying "let's think outside the box" constantly but have a secret concern. You may already know what this is. Don't worry, it is very common. Yes, many managers appreciate the words, but do not know what they mean.

WHOSE BOX? A common worry for managers is that when they use the phrase 'think outside the box' they might be saying something vaguely sexy. Indeed, if you alter the phrase very slightly and ask your team to "think outside my mother's box," then there could be problems. The phrase is not intended to be sexy. The 'box' refers to the established way of thinking. Outside of this box refers to ideas that are not obvious. Some of these 'outside' ideas may be strange, unconventional, stupid or even utterly insane. But this is good.

HOW DO YOU THINK OUTSIDE THE BOX? This really is very simple. All you need to do is weigh up all the possible solutions for a given problem and decide on the best course of action. Once this has been established and agreed, and this is the clever bit, you must do the exact opposite.

Here's an example. Let's say you are with your team, brainstorming a marketing strategy for your newest product. Your team all agree that, as the product is a pharmaceutical which offers a breakthrough in the treatment of AIDS (both good and bad) and that you should target healthcare organisations at home and abroad. A strategy to publicise the product and secure the backing of the relevant organisations is agreed and your team are enthused and motivated.

However, you realise that at no point has anyone thought outside the box. At this point, you should implore the team to think harder. Use the phrase. You may notice that some members of staff will seem uneasy or roll their eyes. Do not be alarmed by this, it is a good sign. It means that the people you manage are not as clever or imaginative as you. At this point you need to assert your leadership. Search for the opposite solution. Insist that a better strategy is to purchase airtime on QVC to sell pills directly to AIDS sufferers. There may be some objections on legal, business or ethical grounds, but do not let this dissuade you. It is a sign that you are truly thinking outside the box and are the same as other 'box rejecters', such as Charles Darwin, Colonel Sanders and James Dyson, who all faced fierce opposition to their ideas which were considered 'outside the box.'

Over the past twenty-two years, the number of written reports has increased by four hundred percent, with information technology being the chief cause. The rise in standards of documentation are also to blame, with managers writing more reports than ever before. Statisticians have worked out that, in a single tax year, the average manager will write over 2.5 million words – the equivalent of writing *War And Peace* five times! Writing reports can be tricky for the modern manager, but here are some tips to turn a chore into a chortle:

ACCURACY. It is a common misnomer that everything you write in a report must be accurate. Although accurate information will give the report's recipient a solid base for decision making, they might not make the right decision that you want them to. Therefore, you are free to write anything that may unfairly persuade your reader. Also, there can be lots of facts and figures to check, and if the answers don't come up in the first three pages of a Google search (nobody looks further than that, except maybe for porn) then feel free to make stuff up.

CONCISENESS. Being concise is over-rated. "If brevity is the soul of wit," said Shakespeare, "then play on. Give me excess of it; that surfeiting, the appetite may quicken, with no lie." In essence, what the great Bard is saying is that concision is an anathema to communication. Writing a report is no different: in fact, it is a fantastic opportunity to show how highly educated you are. Why not mention the similarities between Charles Dickens' *Great Expectations* and your plans for the sales in quarter four, or liken yourself to Hermes, the Greek god of business, when he stole Apollo's cattle? If you speak another language, feel free to casually switch into it, or drop in obscure phrases or posh-sounding words to prove it.

BE CONFIDENT WITH LANGUAGE. Don't worry about spelling or grammar: must spellcheckers wilt catch any errors that you night male. Instead, feel free to really let loose the frustrated novelist inside you – use metaphors daringly with a *soupçon* of inventiveness, and make full use of tangential dream sequences with stream-of-consciousness narratives. You will, however, need to be your own editor. Some words and phrases – such as *basically*, *actually*, *each and every one*, etc – can easily be removed from sentences without changing the meaning or tone, so try leaving each and every one of them out, or removing them entirely. Along with run-on sentences. And starting sentences with and. Be a strong editor, and allow your words to flourish!

212.555.6342

HNTM
Because Those Paradigms
Wont Shift Themselves

Adam KIRKMAN
Vice President

300 EXCHANGE PLACE   NEW YORK   NY 10006   FAX: 312.516.6356   TELEX: 911778 IR

That's bone. The lettering is
something called Cillian Braille.

212.555.6342

HNTM
Because Those Paradigms
Wont Shift Themselves

Daniel **MAYHEW**
Vice President

300 EXCHANGE PLACE   NEW YORK   NY 10006   FAX: 312.516.6356   TELEX: 911778 IR

Eggshell with Romalian type.

212.555.6342

HNTM
BECAUSE THOSE PARADIGMS
WONT SHIFT THEMSELVES

CHRIS **GOODIER**
VICE PRESIDENT

300 EXCHANGE PLACE   NEW YORK   NY 10006   FAX: 312.516.6356   TELEX: 911778 IR

Raised lettering. Pale nimbus. White.

212.555.6342

HNTM
BECAUSE THOSE PARADIGMS
WONT SHIFT THEMSELVES

PAUL **ALLEN**
VICE PRESIDENT

300 EXCHANGE PLACE   NEW YORK   NY 10006
FAX: 312.516.6356   TELEX: 911778 IR

Look at that subtle off-white colouring.
The tasteful thickness of it.
It even has a watermark.

Congratulations, you've just started a new job. You've just been shown around the building and filled in some paperwork for HR. Already, you're thinking about shaking things up. But don't get ahead of yourself. The question you really need to be asking yourself is, how soon can I start working towards my promotion? The answer is, today. Day one is the first day to start. Here are some hints:

ESTABLISH A BOND WITH YOUR BOSS. Your boss will somehow be a buffoon, but you must put aside your incredulity that they were ever promoted to a position of authority at all. The only good decision they ever made was to hire or promote you. They may be physically repulsive or slightly smelly, but don't let these factors be barriers to your eternal friendship. Laugh at their jokes and compliment their dress style. Offer to make them tea or coffee because "I'm making one anyway." (This is also true for popping to the sandwich shop.) Lastly, discover that you have an undying interest in the same things as them, such as Bavarian hat collecting. You may also discover that you follow the same football team, attend the same church, or even went to school together. You may even have been briefly married in the early '90s. Your imagination is the limit.

BE A TEAM PLAYER. Your boss will love it if you profess to be a team player. Perhaps describe all the wonderful team decisions that you were able to facilitate in your previous role as 'team leader', and make sure you mention the word 'team' as much as you can. Profess to adhere to the maxim that "there's no 'I' in team."

ACQUIRE NEW SKILLS. You will be more likely to work your way up a company's structure if you can prove yourself to be valuable as a person. Try impressing people with your bushcraft survival skills, or at least by talking about them. Also, sign yourself up for every training session available. You'll show that you're keen to learn and it's a day out of the office. Besides, once you're there, you can either take over the session, or you can stay at home and lie about going.

CREATE YOUR OWN OPPORTUNITIES. After studying the way the company is run, you may notice that there is a gap in its organisational structure, or there is a potential growth area that has been hitherto ignored. If this is the case, put together a proposal that a senior position be created to handle this oversight, and recommend yourself for the position. Or you can just badmouth your boss to their boss, or stage an accident on the stairs. Don't forget that, to most people, stabbing someone in the back is a metaphor, but to the truly ambitious, it really is literal.

The ability to plan for the long term while maximising performance in the short term is a must for managers. Thinking strategically means affecting the culture, impacting the DNA of the business. Planning strategy means spending a great deal of time thinking, or at least appearing to think. You must remove yourself from the day-to-day grind, perhaps in some kind of controlled, room-serviced environment, and come up with vague plans and unachievable ideas. Be unrealistic. The more unachievable the idea, the better – then you gain plaudits for your high-altitude view, too. Here's how to plan strategy:

ANALYSE, PLAN, IMPLEMENT. There are three stages to building a strategy: analysing, planning, and implementing. Start by analysing where your business is, then plan where you want it to be, and then make sure it gets there. Unfortunately, it's not always that simple. You must remember to analyse your plan, plan your analysis, implement your planning, and analyse the implementation of the plan. Remember to allow enough time to avoid rushing the planning stage, but be sure to know when to move on as over-analysis can lead to paralysis.

START FROM SCRATCH. The Roman philosopher Epictetus told us that "it is impossible for a man to learn what he thinks he already knows." This means that, in order to generate good strategy, you have to forget everything you know. Everything. Make yourself blank like a sheet of paper. Ask yourself some very basic questions, "Are we, or are we not, a business?"

FOCUS. When formulating strategy, it's vital that your focus is right. You may have to ask your hotel for the porn channels to be disabled. Well, that's very specific, but whatever floats your boat. Focus upon the areas in which your business is underperforming, and make alterations to compensate. Simple. For a more in-depth analysis, hire a strategy consultant. If you get a midget or dwarf, try not to think of *Itty Bitty Gang Bang*.

The key point to remember about justifying your decisions is that you do not need to justify yourself to your staff. Ever. Occasionally, however, you may wish to educate your staff in the many ways of your brilliance. Here's how:

DUMB IT DOWN. The employee will already feel out of their depth in discussing such issues of company-wide importance, so it is vital that you explain everything in simple words which are easy to understand. Speak slowly. Depending on the situation, you could draw a diagram, or explain with hand puppets.

BRING EVIDENCE. After making a particularly difficult decision, or perhaps over-ruling an indignant colleague, check the stock prices of your company. If the stock prices have increased by even the smallest amount, then you have made the right decision. If the stock prices happen to have fallen, then you must refer to your high altitude view, or indicate the long-term strategic planning. Say something like "It's better to lose the battle and win the war." Also, you can prove anything by saying "Fact!" after it. Fact.

BE PHILOSOPHICAL. Your staff naturally would never be able to comprehend the plane you are operating on, and you should avoid trying to explain this to them for their own sake. Instead, offer a glimpse into your genius with a well-judged slice of philosophy. Here's an example. You are coaching an individual who is asking you why you decided to award a bonus to the entire department apart from her. Look her in the eye, lean towards her and whisper, "A journey of a thousand miles starts with a single footstep."

You may find that when you start explaining your decisions to your staff that you experience a strange and unwelcome sensation. This is the feeling that you have no idea why you made the decisions that you did. Do not be alarmed. Rather than indicating that you do not know what you are doing, it indicates a much more positive development. You have reached such a level of professional artistry and instinctive brilliance that you unthinkingly make brilliant decisions without any conscious effort! You are so good at your job that thinking does not weigh you down. Remember, in management, thinking is your enemy. Do tigers think? No. Do eagles think? No. Did dodos think? Yes, and now they are dead.

Despite your obvious managerial prowess, it seems that bad news is never too far away. Bad news can come in many forms and disguises, but the golden rule of dealing with bad news is that it is never your fault, even if the evidence disagrees. If this is the case, then you must ignore the problem until someone raises the issue, and then it becomes their fault. In either situation, it invariably falls to you to *carpe* the *diem* in order to rescue the situation.

The key to doing this lies in how you deal with the bad news. Psychologists have researched this, and the Kübler-Ross model indicates that when you receive bad news, you pass through five stages:

DENIAL. There is no need for you to pass through this stage. As a manager, you are one step ahead of your troops at all times, which means you have already taken the first step of any solution.

ANGER. The importance of this stage cannot be misunderestimated. Getting angry shows you are passionate about your job and committed to its success. It helps to throw things or slam objects, but refrain from hitting staff unless you can be absolutely sure your violence will ensure their silence.

BARGAINING. Bargaining is a very powerful tool in the manager's arsenal. Some psychologists believe that the bargaining stage is ultimately ineffective as you cannot bargain with the bad news. However, we paid some other psychologists to agree with us that bargaining can be effective. Remember, bargaining is just a fancy word for blackmail.

DEPRESSION. Depression is a mental illness, which means it is psychosomatic. This is a technical term for 'made-up', like M.E. It is a simple fact of life that depression can be overcome with alcohol.

ACCEPTANCE. The final stage in dealing with bad news is acceptance. The quicker you accept bad news, the better you are. Feel free to skip any stages that you think would interfere in your own progress. Perhaps be so *laissez-faire* that you appear not to give a shit. Now, that's good management.

The 80:20 rule dictates that eighty percent of your output comes from twenty percent of your input. This is sometimes known as the Pareto Principle, named after the Italian economist Vilfredo Pareto who noticed that 80% of Italy's wealth was in the hands of 20% of the population. This wild discrepancy forms the basis of the 80:20 rule.

Simply put, the goal when using the 80:20 rule is to maximise the small and powerful 20% of your time to increase the output from it. Why not spend more than 20% of your time on this small but powerful 20% of your time?

Here are a few ways to use the rule to your advantage:

80 + 20 = 100. This can be simply demonstrated on a pie chart, and also makes it easy to work out percentages. So

if you effectively use 20% of your time to create 80% of your output, you will generate 100% profit.

ELIMINATION. The concept behind the 80:20 rule is that you concentrate on the 20% which is most effective, and therefore decrease the time you spend ineffectively. If you apply this rule ad infinitum, so that you are always reducing the amount of time that you spend ineffectively, then you will eventually end up with nothing. This means that you have finished your job and you can retire.

PERFECTIONISM. Say, for example, that it takes you two years to learn to play the guitar, and after those two years you are 80% competent at this, but to gain that last 20% of competency, you must invest a further eight years of time in training. The 80:20 rule dictates that this is not a fair use of your time – you are already 80% good at the guitar in only two years, so why bother wasting a further eight years getting perfect? You can apply this principle across the board so that you need only demonstrate the most rudimentary levels of skill at any particular task to declare yourself 80% competent, and as we've already seen, 80 + 20 = 100, so you're instantly an expert at everything. But you knew that already.

As a manager, it's your job to make tough decisions which can have far-ranging implications. Sometimes, you're torn between two options. Now usually, you just flip a coin, but there's people watching, you can't get away and they need an answer ASAP. Perhaps people are telling you different things and you don't know whose opinion to trust. Luckily, we have some hints and tips for you in this department.

TRUST. Now, it doesn't matter what the opinion is, it matters who the giver of the opinion is. For example, it might not sound like a particularly good idea, but if it comes from your boss, then that's the idea to go with. If it sounds like a great idea, but it comes from someone you don't really like, then that's not the way forward for you. If you work with your spouse, then it's advisable that you agree with them on everything, unless you're having an affair and want to end it all anyway. The same is true of working with relatives. But not the affair bit, obviously.

THE PETER PRINCIPLE. In every organisation, employees who are competent at their jobs are promoted. Eventually, however, they reach a level at which their competence ceases. Anything that works will be used in progressively more challenging arenas until its competency fails. This is known as the Peter Principle – that employees always rise to their level of incompetence, and are then stuck there. (This concept doesn't apply to you, however, as your name isn't Peter. If it is, then sorry Pete – you're stuck in your current job.) But, I hear you ask, how does this help me decide whose opinion to trust? Quite simply, you must ignore the advice of those who have been caught in the Peter Principle – anyone who has been promoted several times, or anyone who has been there for years. Taking the Peter Principle to its full extent, all the real work is done by people who have yet to reach their level of incompetence. These are the people to be trusted – people who've never been promoted, or shown any skills, foresight or judgement. These are the go-getting folk whose opinions you must trust.

WHO DO YOU AGREE WITH? Although you're kind of torn about what decision to make, deep down you have a gut feeling about what's right. Psychologists state that once you've made a decision, you either feel peace with it (indicating that you think it's the right one) or you worry about it (indicating that you think it's wrong.) Why not make a snap decision over a difficult choice? See how you feel about it once you've decided. You can always change your mind, and then change it back – as many times as you want. Your staff won't mind this.

How To Master Sarcasm

Psychologists have found a worryingly deep link between sarcasm and aggression, believing that people use sarcasm as a means of indirectly expressing aggression towards others as well as revealing insecurities about themselves. People will also tell you that 'sarcasm is the lowest form of wit.' But they're just tossers and you're allowed to punch them. Sarcasm is brilliant, and here's how to master it:

THE GOLDEN RULE. The trouble with sarcasm is that there is a fine line between a joke and an insult. You will need to learn the difference to allow your workplace to be just as much fun as you are. Although sarcasm can be complicated – sometimes, *sarcastic comments mean the exact opposite of what they appear to mean!* – we have a golden rule which allows you to differentiate between a jovial sarcastic comment and an unacceptable insult. The golden rule is this: if you say something sarcastically to a colleague, then it is true sarcasm at its finest. However, if a colleague says something sarcastic about you, then it is a deliberate and scurrilous insult.

KNOW YOUR AUDIENCE. You have to judge the sarchasm of your audience – the gap between those who use sarcasm and those who fail to understand it. After spending time with people, you will gauge their sense of humour, and you can pitch your sarcastic comment just right. The only exception to this rule is with total strangers – be as dryly sarcastic as you desire, preferably on topics of race, gender or religion. They will respect your healthy sense of humour, and if they're offended, then they're clearly secretly racist or sexist. Well, duh, it's sarcasm, retard.

SCAN BEFORE YOU SEND. Sarcasm often doesn't come across well when written down, so you must be careful to indicate when you are being sarcastic. (This helps decrease the sarchasm.) If you're not sure that your sarcasm is coming across, don't leave it out. Why not try overloading your text, email, document or presentation with stupid smiley-faced emoticons?

"Failure is the opportunity to begin again, more intelligently," said Henry Ford, which is easy to say when you only made one type of car! The demands on today's managers are so much greater than on yesteryear's entrepreneurs. Even though you have told people that they are to be successful, sometimes they're not, and as such you will occasionally have to deal with failure. If it looks like something you're involved in will fail, don't get bogged down in trying to save it, you should instead begin to distance yourself from it immediately. Begin to apportion blame – this is the golden rule. Someone, somewhere, is at fault. Find them and single them out. But how else can you deal with failure?

LEARN YOUR LESSON. Winston Churchill said that "Success is going from one failure to another with no loss of enthusiasm." You can achieve this easily! Don't lose any enthusiasm. In fact, don't change anything about yourself. If you do everything the same, it's statistically more likely to work out favourably this time.

FAILURE IS GOOD? Recently, there has been a growing trend in business circles to treat failure as a positive thing. Some people say the person who doesn't make any mistakes is unlikely to make anything at all. Some people believe that failure is a major contributor to success. These people are stupid! Failure is obviously bad. Try to avoid failure as much as possible.

"FAILURE IS NOT AN OPTION." Make it clear to your team that failure is unacceptable. If people know that they can't rely on falling back on failure then they'll work harder. This isn't denial, it's, um, well it just isn't denial. Be sure to use *Apollo 13*'s sound bite to inspire your employees. Say it as often as possible. You can even do the Yank accent if you want, but be careful not to get confused with another Tom Hanks movie. You don't want to give a rousing battle cry to your troops and end it with "My momma always said stupid is as stupid does," or "AIDS is a deadly, incurable disease." If you do get it mixed up, don't worry. Life's like that sometimes. It's not the end of the world. Just pass round some chocolates.

Answer the following questions as honestly as you can. Each question asks you whether this is true of you. Award yourself points for the following:

1. Never, 2. Occasionally, 3. Often, 4. Always.

Add up your scores and refer to the guide at the end.

1 I focus on details and find that nothing is too trivial to dwell on.

2 I show an active interest in my employees by covertly monitoring their emails and telephone calls.

3 I am flexible in approach and am willing to hurt staff if it benefits the business.

4 I am open to criticism but know not to take any notice of it.

5 I feel uncomfortable outside work because people do not know how important I am, so I must tell them.

6 I do not get bogged down in details like doing actual work and prefer to walk around shouting and pointing.

I am a creative thinker and always find the best way to bully an employee into leaving.

 I am not afraid to powerdress for success and I get my hair done at Toni & Guy. I understand that nothing impresses others more than my big gold watch.

 I am future-focused and do not waste time on that important thing that someone said five minutes ago.

 I am aware of my achievements and strengths and make time to list my achievements and strengths to my staff whenever I can.

SCORES 1-10. You have much scope to improve your management style but you show some promise. Perhaps put the crayons down, and try using a biro.

SCORES 11-20. You prick. You disgust us. You don't even have the decency to be completely crap like the retards we patronised in the 1-10 section. Now get out.

SCORES 21-30. You are almost there. You clearly have the potential to reach the level you need. Focus on your focus. Ask yourself – what is my focus? Is it in focus?

SCORES 31-40. You have got it. You talk the talk and walk the walk. You have the right stuff. We like your style. Come work for us, champ. Now.

ASK YOURSELF...

"IS THIS WORKPLACE
BEING ALL IT CAN BE?"

ASK YOURSELF...

"IS THIS AN
EMPOWERING
ENVIRONMENT?"

STEP TWO:

HOW TO IMPROVE OFFICE LIFE

IS THIS WORKPLACE BEING ALL IT CAN BE?

Your entire company may not be achieving everything it could be. While it's highly unlikely that this is personally your fault, anything's possible. You need to ensure that your workplace is being all it can be. Improving office life is all down to you. Now, this isn't easy. Offices of all sizes operate like a difficult and complex machine, with thousands of delicate moving parts all interacting perfectly to achieve coherence. Tinkering with this machine can have extreme effects. You must think carefully about the possible effects of any changes that you might make and decide if it is in the best interests of the office to make them. Alternatively, however, this next section offers some quick-fix solutions to improving office life.

IS THIS AN EMPOWERING ENVIRONMENT?

It's your job as a modern manager to create a culture in which the workforce can grow and flourish in the office environment. You need to be impacting the DNA, bringing massive change to every aspect of the company's culture. You need to make the environment empowering. Are you up for the challenge? Don't worry if you're not, just buy some fake plants and stick them in reception, and devour the knowledge of this next section.

So you want to bond with the lads? To gain their trust, respect and admiration? This is really quite straightforward once you realise what men are all about. Men like three things: football, women and drinking. Some people will tell you that men are more diverse and complex than this, and in some cases - say Gandhi, Nietzsche or Jesus - this may be true. You could take an approach which respects this diversity and individuality, but let's face it, it sounds really hard and would probably take ages. So forget that, all men respect a manager who knows about football, is a hit with the ladies and can drink everyone under the table. Here are some top tips:

FOOTBALL. If there is a five-a-side team, join it immediately. In fact, insist that you become the centre forward, captain and manager, as your men will respect you for this decisiveness. Pick the team, berate underachievers and tell them all that you once had a trial at Plymouth (Plymouth is good because no-one will check it out). You may find that some players will leave the team and you may vaguely hear a few insults aimed at you just out of earshot. Don't let this concern you. This is a sign that you are winning them over. If there is no five-a-side team, start one and make it mandatory for all male staff to attend matches. Then only pick the good ones to leave the others with shattered self-confidence because, hey, it's all about winning. Also, it doesn't matter if you're rubbish at football – you can always blame the pitch, ball, weather or referee.

 THE LADIES. A good technique here is to make sexual comments about female workers when you are in the presence of your male staff. Say things like, "I definitely would," or, "She's a five-pinter, eh lads?" Men love this kind of banter. You can also ask them about their wives' and girlfriends' sexual proclivities. They may appear resistant but will have you marked as a real player and be full of admiration. Make sure to tell them about any conquests of your own in great detail (or, if you've been too busy at the office, make them up) and if you're married, boast about having loads of affairs. You may notice a few men looking vaguely disgusted or even nauseated. Do not let this stop you, psychologists state that impressed men often display these behaviours.

DRINKING. Find out where your male staff go drinking after work by monitoring their emails or phone calls, then delight them by turning up unannounced, sitting yourself down and talking shop. If they seem to go a bit quiet take this as your cue to talk more. Perhaps describe the Quarter 3 sales figures and ask for ideas about how to improve them. If you don't get much of a response, get a round or two in and just keep talking. Remember to get louder and louder as the evening goes on.

How To Bond
With The Girls: For Men

We live in changing times. The feminist movement of the 1970s produced widespread changes in attitude towards women in the workplace and gave all women hope that they could one day be treated as a man's equal. And while feminism is all well and good, it's not going to get the washing up done, is it? What these changes mean for a male manager is that you must *at all times* pretend that you value your female staff as much as their male colleagues. A vital part of creating this pretence is bonding with the girls. Here's how to do it.

KNOW YOUR ENEMY. Women are an infinitely complex range of individuals with amazing abilities and skills in different areas of life. They can bring perspectives that can completely alter the way you see the world. Some of them are even competent at their jobs. To understand them, it is useful to try to see the world from a female viewpoint. But how do women think? The answer is, they don't. Scientists have proved that women are automatons driven by the toxic cocktail of hormones swirling around their poor little heads. To bond with them, you should remember this. While you and your male staff are thinking about this month's profit and loss forecasts, your female staff will all be thinking about Brangelina. Oh, and all women generalise. All of them.

THEY ALL FANCY YOU. An important fact to understand as a male manager is that every single one of your female staff will want to sleep with you. It's not their fault: they are programmed to be attracted to their superiors. Keep them happy with regular winks, lascivious comments or pat them on the bottom as they pass you in the corridor. Or why not make a clumsy move on them at the Christmas party? Tell them your wife doesn't understand you, but they do. They will appreciate that.

MATERNITY LEAVE. A sad fact about all women is that no matter how committed they are to their job they will all, without exception, swan off on maternity leave. All women are morbidly obsessed with babies. Brangelina aside, they think of little else. Legislation says that you should not treat them any differently because of this, but don't worry about that. Legislation is really only a suggestion: it's not compulsory.

Show an interest in babies. Show pregnant women that you care about their welfare by asking them at least once a day if they feel alright and if they want to go off on maternity leave yet. Perhaps ask them if they have haemorrhoids or bladder problems. If you have any female staff that are not pregnant, be sure to ask them why not. Women are baby crazy. They will welcome your interest and feel that you really understand what makes them tick. The advantage of this is that it makes them confused and less likely to take you to a tribunal when you constructively dismiss them for being pregnant.

Unfortunately for women, becoming an expert on football, the ladies and drinking are not going to help you bond with the lads. They may assume you are a lesbian, and not in a good way. A wholly different approach is required. Research indicates that there is one kind of woman a man respects above all others: their mum. So the approach for female managers is to smother your male staff in mothering.

But what does this mean in real terms? Here are some pointers:

OFFER SUPPORT. Tell them that they can always come and talk to you about any concerns they may have. Use a phrase like, "My door is always open." They hopefully won't take you up on this but if they do, refer the tearful loser on to Human Resources. They'll know what to do.

ASSUME THEY ARE STUPID. This takes men right back to childhood where psychologists have proved things. Important things. You may wish to pore over every detail of what they do and find fault again and again. Psychologists have almost certainly said important things about this at some point, too.

DON'T BE AFRAID TO PATRONISE. This is really important in bonding with male staff. While some of them may have hopes, dreams and interests outside of work, it really is unlikely. If they do something well, tell them they show promise and that if they continue they may make sub-assistant team supervisor within five years. Also, make comments like, "It's all beer money to you!" or, "Did you see that Ferrari on *Top Gear* last night?"

In some cases, you may find yourself with an individual male member of staff who, no matter what, just doesn't seem able to bond with you. Unfortunately, this can happen. If it does happen to you, do not panic, just shag him.

How To Bond
With The Girls: For Women

A female manager can enjoy a bond with her female staff which is almost mystical in its beauty. Shared understandings can create a near psychic bond between female manager and female underling. You should strive to create such a bond with all of your women staff.

If that doesn't work though, just destroy the vixens before they destroy you. Here are some things to take into account:

THEY ALL WANT TO BE JUST LIKE YOU. Remember that for your female staff, you are the living embodiment of everything they would like to be. You have more power, a better car and bigger shoulder pads than they could ever dream to have. While it's possible that one or two individuals may want something different out of life, let's face it, it's unlikely. They want to be you, and you should encourage this. Start sentences with, "When I was your age..." whenever you can.

BE HONEST. Your female staff will enjoy little more than hearing about your personal life. They will be desperate to know more about you. Be as open as you like. If you have had a row with your husband, tell them. If you have diarrhoea, tell them. If you are having a clandestine affair with the Financial Director, tell them. Give as much detail as you can.

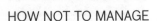

BECOME AN EXPERT IN FASHION. All women like shoes, handbags and dresses. Dress to impress, and be sure to judge your co-workers' attire. Tell everyone what you think.

KILL OR BE KILLED. Not all your female employees will be useful to you. It is very important that in the Machiavellian snake pit of the modern workplace, you identify and exterminate any threat. Dumpy women are fine, they can stay, and the same goes for stupid women. However, you must single out and destroy all the female staff who are more attractive or more intelligent than you. If you don't, they will steal your job. But how is this done? Bully them ruthlessly.

USE NATURE. As an addendum, it is worth noting that if a group of women spends enough time together, their menstrual cycles synchronise. This is the ultimate sign that you have bonded with your female staff, so be sure to ask them loudly in mixed company if it is their "time of the month" when you are on. You may want to use a humorous euphemisticism like "surfing the crimson wave" or "being visited by Aunt Flo." If one of your staff is post-menopausal, then don't feel the need to bond with them on this. Nature has discarded them, and so can you. If you are successful in synchronising your cycles, then you have truly bonded with your female staff.

How To Deal With Homosexuality In The Workplace

For the purposes of this entry, the term 'gay' will include those who are bisexual, gay and lesbian, just because it's a bit simpler that way. The first thing to make clear is that there is nothing wrong with being a gay, which is why there is an entry in this guide detailing *How To Deal With Heterosexuality In The Workplace*. Being a gay is simply being part of a sexual minority, like S&M fetishism, and paedophilia. Remember, the golden rule is that gays are people too.

Here are a few tips to dealing with their kind:

BEING OUT WITH WORK COLLEAGUES. Try as we might, society still attaches a certain stigma to being a gay. This leads some gays to hide their sexuality from their work colleagues, which can lead to depression and severe hissy fits. The modern office must be a place where a gay can feel comfortable to be 'out'. Try to encourage potential gays to out themselves by appearing open to discussing literature, plays and *Sex And The City*.

DETECTING THE GAYS. Heterosexuals have a primitive form of 'gaydar' – you are able to detect gays by their declaration of love for musical theatre, or their strange distaste of football but interest in footballers – but this is not an iron-clad way of detecting a gay. Only gays have truly effective 'gaydar', and you will need to recruit one to allow you to detect the others.

FLY LIKE EAGLES. When an eaglet is in the nest, they are warm, comfortable and protected – and therefore reluctant to leave. It takes a little push for them to tumble from the nest in order to learn that they have wings, and can soar. The same is true of gays. Sometimes, they just need to be 'outed.' (Why not copy relatives in on the inter-departmental 'outing' e-mail?) Eventually, they will give you a mincing thanks for your role in allowing them to soar.

A colleague is surprised, but grateful, to hear news of his 'outing.'

USING THE WORD 'GAY' IN CONVERSATION. It is perfectly acceptable to use the word 'gay' in ordinary conversation without fear of PC reprisals. The term had its first phase of meaning back in the Victorian days, meaning happy, and it then passed through its second phase during the late '80s and early '90s, meaning homosexual, and has now passed into its third phase, meaning a little bit "meh."

As such, it is acceptable to refer to bad news as "gay" or to refer to a colleague's irritating behaviour as "being gay." However, there are derogatory terms for the gays, and you must be careful not to refer to a gay by one of these insulting terms when they are in earshot – so avoid terms like rugmuncher, fudge packer, muff diver, vulva vulture, backshot artist, brownpipe engineer, chocolate chimney sweeper, mangina lover, nut administrator, poopdeck penis pumper, rump ranger, sausage jockey, stool stuffer, turd burglar and vagetarian. These derogatory terms have no place in the modern orifice.

METROSEXUALS. These are individuals who are sexually attracted to the Mini Metro. They fantasise about the exhaust pipe of this small car, manufactured by MG between 1980 and 1994. Metrosexuals do it in the garage. While this may seem like an unusual sexual preference, try to hide your disgust. It must be remembered that as with the gays, what metrosexuals do in the privacy of their own home is solely between them and our Lord.

A NOTE ON LESBIANS. In researching this book, the authors found that there are a huge amount of low-to-mid-budget films which focus on lesbianism, with particular emphasis on the nature of the most intimate aspects of lesbians' physical relationships. It seems that, contrary to stereotypes, all lesbians are young, attractive and mainly work in the nursing profession. To find out more, the authors (individually) sat through nearly five hundred hours of such footage. We concluded that lesbians are totally and utterly awesome.

As a homosexual manager, you may be lucky enough to manage a team made up only of homosexuals. However, if you don't work in the fashion industry or for Arsenal Football Club, it is likely that many of your team will sadly be heterosexuals. These sick individuals have many strange characteristics, but you must cope somehow. Here are some pointers:

HETEROSEXUALS ARE NOTORIOUSLY PROMISCUOUS. While stereotypes can be inaccurate, this one isn't. Most heterosexuals have had many different sexual partners, sometimes outside of a loving relationship. If there happens to be a heterosexual man and a heterosexual woman in your team, they will definitely end up having sex together. They can't help themselves.

HOW TO SPOT A HETEROSEXUAL. It is very easy to spot a heterosexual man. As well as displaying the trophies of their sexuality (such as children) they are all, without exception, totally lame. They buy their clothes in Next and many don't even moisturise, let alone exfoliate. Many have never even seen *Calamity Jane*. Heterosexual women are generally alright and will think you are just fabulous. They're very good at gossip and watch *Ugly Betty*.

THE NAKED WOMAN FETISHIST. Many heterosexual men can get aroused simply by seeing an unclothed woman. In fact, they find it hard to get aroused by anything else! These kind of men may spend hours sat in front of the TV, flicking through the channels in the hope of seeing a naked breast which, for many of these fetishists, is sufficient to create a sexual thrill.

For some, it becomes an all-consuming obsessive disorder and these twisted individuals find themselves spending work time at work when they should be working at work simply wondering what their female co-workers would look like in the buff. Seek these sick fiends out and sack them!

Morale is one of the trickiest thorns that the modern manager can ever have to pull from the paw of the weeping lion. Despite your wonderful leadership, some people are not happy. The question you then need to ask yourself is "We need to improve morale. What program can we introduce that doesn't cost much, or preferably anything?"

Luckily, morale is now quantifiable. Scientists have found a complicated way to measure the morale of a workforce – using Field-Operated Numerical Zones – and have found that a happy workplace averages 30 megaFONZies. If your office isn't that happy, then you can use the following top tips to improve morale:

COMMUNICATE THE SUCCESS! Let the staff know just how successful the company is. Perhaps you can speak about the profits the board have made, or the bonus you have just received.

GIVE THEM A SUGGESTION BOX. This is a wonderful way for staff to offer tips on how you can improve their working life. The only downside is that a few bad apples can use this as an excuse to say awful things due to the anonymity involved. The obvious answer is to put the box outside your office, or have it watched on CCTV. Empty it every fifteen minutes. Study handwriting samples. When you know exactly who said what, you can retaliate as necessary.

TEAMBUILDING EXERCISES. These can be a mixture of external jaunts, or office-bound activities, such as office golf, desk tennis, or kitchen utensil Jenga. It's vital that attendance is compulsory. You can only build morale as long as everyone attends. Except maybe those miserable sods that would just grumble all the way through. Leave them behind to answer the phone.

LEAD BY EXAMPLE. Leaders should be seen enjoying their work! Walk round with a permanent Cheshire grin. Remember, if the sides of your face don't hurt, then you're not smiling enough. Be known as the "fun-loving" boss. Effortlessly create laughter and relaxation in the workplace. Why not institute a fancy dress Friday, or forward on some humorous emails, or bring your guitar to work?

How To Interview For New Staff

Interviewing for new staff can be tricky. You only have a limited amount of time to decide whether the candidate is capable of doing the job, as well as considering how well they would fit into the existing team. Candidates will give you answers that sound good and may even seem to be excellent potential employees.

You need to see through such obvious attempts to win you over, and get to the crux of the matter as soon as possible: deciding if, at some point in the future, they will ever sleep with you. Remember, you can hire someone just because you fancy them - studies show that attractive people are more likely to be hired or promoted. Sometimes, however, the field is not up to scratch, not even an 'office pretty' amongst the beasts. In that case, here are some handy hints to interviewing:

THE FIRST FIVE SECONDS ARE VITAL. It's true to say that in these first five seconds, you will already have made your mind up whether or not they have the job. If this really is the case, call an end to the interview right there: if they have been successful, let them know immediately. If they have not been successful, don't let them sit down, just explain there's been a misunderstanding, and show them the door. If you are unsure after the first five seconds, then you can continue with the interview. Remember to keep a straight face and interview them seriously, even if they're obese, disabled or an ethnic.

READ BETWEEN THE LINES. Be aware that interviewees will probably lie to you, or at the least embellish the truth in order to make themselves seem more appealing to employers. You may need to read between the lines – a gap year, or time spent "travelling", is usually a euphemism for frequenting an opium den in China, or for jail time.

DEALING WITH LIARS. A sad fact is that everyone you interview will be lying. This is understandable, really, because of course they're crap, they're hardly going to be as brilliant as you, are they? The interviewee is the enemy and your agenda should be to catch them out. Accuse them of lying, and grill them on petty details. Test their knowledge by saying something like "I see you got an 'A' in GCSE Geography. So, how is an oxbow lake formed?" or "You achieved a 'B' in dual science. What are the characteristics of a noble gas?"

A common mistake for managers to make is to ask straightforward and clear questions such as, "What do you consider to be your key strengths?" or "Where do you see yourself in five years?" Never ask these kinds of questions because they will be expecting them and will have rehearsed the answers! You should be creative with your questions. Think outside the box! Ask yourself – will they have been expecting this question? If the answer is 'never in a million years' – then you are on the right track. For example, instead of asking them to tell you what kind of person they are, why not ask, "If you could choose someone to sit next to on a long-haul flight, who would it be?" or, "If you were an animal, what other animal would you eat and why?" or, "If you were trapped in a burning bus with a nun, a tiger and a bottle opener, would you smash a window to get out or wait for the emergency services?" They will never expect this approach and their answer will speak volumes. You may not know what the answer means, but never mind. It will speak volumes.

TREAT IT LIKE TV. Imagine you're a TV detective interviewing a suspect. Play good cop, bad cop. Try to intimidate them. Smoke at them. Perhaps even go renegade. Put your swipe card down and say something like "There are no managers here now. It's just you and me, *mano y mano*..."

From time to time, you will find that members of staff leave your little family. This usually occurs after you have managed to teach them everything that they can learn from you, which is why they usually cite you as their reason for leaving. This leaves you in the unenviable position of having to recruit new members of staff. But how do you go about this?

Ask around. Make casual enquiries with your staff to see if they know anyone who is looking for a new job. Hiring friends, partners, relatives or exes makes your search strategy simple. Plus, there will be no problem integrating them into existing teams, as they'll already know someone! This technique is 100% guaranteed not to backfire, for example with staff treating work time as an extension of their social life, or by putting lovers in the same team.

Advertise. This may be as simple as a sign in the window, or perhaps you will need to advertise in a newspaper or through a trade magazine. Most job advertising is done on the internet now, either through dedicated job websites or on a company's official website. Just Google the word 'job'.

Job descriptions. For god's sake avoid the common mistake of specifying what the job involves. If you do, you will regret it when some whining loser comes to you office to tell you that, "this isn't the job I applied for." Be as vague as you can. Avoiding specifics at all costs is the golden rule of looking for new staff.

SALARIES. You may face a dilemma here. You want to get good staff but you don't want to pay them a good salary. Be creative. There's a magic phrase you can use here: "Up to." For example, "remuneration up to £70k." You know the salary on offer is only £12k, but you'll only get idiots or women applying for a job with a salary of £12,000!

Some candidates may question this discrepancy. If they do, make something up about bonuses or 'on target earnings.' That will be enough to fool them.

HOW TO AVOID UNSUITABLE CANDIDATES. Unfortunately, it is illegal to specify 'no fat mingers' in a job advert, but there is a way around this. Facebook! Be aware that searching for candidates' profiles on Facebook is unethical, and if you want to be technical about it, stalking, but it will pay off handsomely.

Simply look them up to assess their aesthetic suitability for your organisation. This way you can weed out fat, ugly or foreign people, or people with children. Note that if a candidate has a profile picture of scenery or their dog they are definitely mingers and you can discount them.

And if you come across a photo of a slamming hottie looking hammered and doing tequila shots from the breasts of her equally attractive female friend, get them in for an interview *tout de suite*!

HEADHUNT. Don't be confused! This does not mean hiring a maniac to decapitate people, or doing it yourself with a hatchet and the music of *Huey Lewis and The News*. No, headhunting refers to the practice of seeking out excellent employees from other companies and offering them a substantial pay rise to defect to your company. This is an excellent way of boosting your business and crippling your competition. You can also headhunt young, smart individuals straight from colleges and universities. The great thing about students is that you get older, but they stay the same age.

The modern manager is increasingly being called to either lead teams or work as part of one in order to achieve company goals. This can be irritating because it means you actually have to work in close proximity with your staff, which is understandably trying. Similarly, teamwork poses the risk that you might be caught out and actually have to do some real work. Luckily, we have Five Cs for Working In Teams:

CLEAR EXPECTATIONS. Any team needs clear expectations set out for them, otherwise they do not know what they need to achieve. How can you score if you don't have a goal? As a manager, it is your duty to set out these objectives. Do not wait for the group to decide them – this is not a democracy. Dictate the demands right at the start so that everyone is singing from the same hymn sheet. Alternatively, don't. Then you can blame the group for being directionless.

CONTEXT. It is important that team members know why they are on the team. Only when they understand their role in the group will each individual play their part in the team's glorification. Don't be afraid to stereotype when picking your team – make sure you have a nerd for the technical stuff, a blonde for tea-making (and eye candy!), an overkeen enthusiast to do all the work, and all the necessary racial and sexual minorities to avoid lawsuits.

COMMITMENT. Team members need to be committed to the group. You should regularly test their commitment by demanding unpaid overtime and insist they demonstrate their loyalty by fire-walking. If you don't have the budget for a fire-walk, or you just want to do it in the office, you can either use scattered drawing pins or simply get them to hold scalding hot tea.

COLLABORATION. This is perhaps the key to all group work: the ability to work in groups. Without this, teams would flounder as they are merely individuals and not teams. No single individual has ever won a World Cup, or a World War. Collaboration, or teamwork, is the most important factor in working in teams.

COMMUNICATION. One of the cornerstones of collaboration, and hence teamwork, is communication. This can often be difficult when working in large groups. Make sure you finish other people's sentences. Talk over them if necessary. You may want to start their sentences, too. Talk loudly.

By concentrating on these five areas of teamwork, you have ensured that the team has contributed most effectively to the success of the business. Your team members will love you, your business will soar, and you will have created empowered employees who are responsible for their work processes. Can your work life get any better?

Every business has, at some point, to deal with customers. Conventional business techniques teach us that the customer is the focus of the business and that employees should strive to satisfy them.

However, conventional businesses are failing every day, so this is clearly a tactic that does not pay dividends. So we recommend treating the customer like shit. Sure, you may lose the odd customer, but if you visualise your customer like the type of woman who always picks a bastard, or the kind of guy who always chases after a bitch, then you'll realise there are some customers who'll never leave you, even if you beat them.

COMPLAINTS PROCEDURE. From time to time though, this policy can lead to complaints, and they can't all be fixed with a nice dinner and a promise to change. The best way to deal with complaints is to create a complaints procedure that is incomprehensible and infuriating. Perhaps give out an invalid e-mail address for people to contact, or construct an elaborate phone system with voice recognition software that repeats back the word "terrific" instead of "terrible" and "affable" for "awful." Placing people on hold with a MIDI rendition of Robbie Williams' *Rock DJ* is also a winner.* Techniques like these ensure that most people's anger will have blown itself out by the time they actually get around to complaining.

PLAY THE GAME. It is a widely believed fact that an unhappy customer will tell twenty-five people that they received poor service, whereas a happy customer will only tell five people how pleased they are. These odds are not in your favour, no matter how excellent your customer service is. Therefore the most effective solution is to badmouth the competition, thus making your own company appear better by comparison.

GET INVOLVED. You may also want to take this opportunity to undermine your staff. If an employee is dealing with a complaint, and they are handling it according to company policy and doing so with grace, feel free to steam in and pay the customer off. Apologise profusely for your staff's incompetence, preferably in front of them – they need to learn. The customer is satisfied, having learned the lesson that causing a fuss works, and the employee is happy to have learnt their place in the hierarchy. Good managing!

* Get yours at http://tinyurl.com/5cdopb today.

The world has experienced many terrible events in the last few years such as the Boxing Day Tsunami of 24th December 2004, and the devastation of New Orleans by Katrina and the Waves in 2005. As bad as these events were, they were nothing compared to the terror and devastation caused by the current Credit Crunch. The value of houses has plummeted. In many areas, houses are now no longer obscenely over-priced, but merely grossly over-priced. This horrific collapse of the housing market has had a knock-on effect on consumer confidence and things look bleak. Everyone is worried. So how do you manage your team in these hard times?

CUT COSTS. (Also see *How To Save Costs*.) These are certainly terrifying times for managers like you and belt-tightening is the order of the day. A manager we know has been forced to meet his mistresses at a Travel Lodge instead of a Holiday Inn! We have heard of other managers having to trade in their BMW X5s for BMW X3s. However, you should not do this. These managers found that driving these inferior vehicles had a devastating effect on staff morale. Remember, your staff view you as a god. Ask yourself – what kind of god would drive an X3? That's right, a rubbish one.

REDUNDANCY IS YOUR FRIEND. This beautiful process has been getting managers out of scrapes for decades, and it keeps on giving. The Credit Crunch can do its worst, but you can always downsize your team. Some staff may not see the big picture and selfishly have a negative view towards being made redundant, citing problems with paying their mortgage and feeding their families. Boo hoo. You may, of course, be concerned that your own position is under threat and you could yourself be downsized. Many experts suggest planning for such a possibility by putting money aside, exploring other career opportunities and the like. These experts, however, are wrong. If you plan for redundancy that's what you'll get. It's a self-fulfilling prophecy. Much better to put your fingers in your ears and carry on.

HELP IS ON THE WAY. Nowhere is the Credit Crunch causing more concern than in Ethiopia. Worried sick about the decline in new mortgage approvals and high street spending in Britain, the people of Ethiopia have put their own problems to one side and started a charity, CrunchAid. In October 2008, CrunchAid staged a fund-raising concert in Addis Ababa featuring four of the country's top performers and entertainers. Headlining the concert was Adebe 'Mr Stick' Tassema who has his own stick which he held aloft to the delight of the crowd.

Attendance was disappointing, which organisers put down to the widespread famine, civil war, disease and death which have been raging across the country for the last thirty years. However, they were able to raise the equivalent of almost half of Ethiopia's annual GDP to help British homeowners. The bad news is that this £12.87 will not last forever.

Why have a mission statement? You must have a mission statement. This is absolutely, crucially, integrally paramount. When writing your mission statement, be sure to avoid anything that is specific or indeed has any meaning at all. Remember, specifics create problems!

For example, if you write that you will become the biggest wholesale retailer of medical grade hosiery in the Hove area by the end of the decade you will actually have to do it! Much better to use vague platitudes. Why not write, "We are committed in our belief that every individual in the Hove area needs medical grade hosiery in their life. We are committed to seek out every opportunity to bring our products to those who need them."

Writing a mission statement can be a terrifically complicated task. The resulting article should encapsulate the aims and ethics of your business, as well as setting out measurable objectives which you can refer to in years to come. Although this sounds like a potential rod for your back – what happens when your actions oppose the ethical guidelines you set down? What if you haven't achieved your objectives? – we luckily have some useful tips to writing the perfect mission statement.

Should your company already have an existing mission statement, then you should re-write it. People will be impressed by your forward-thinking, can-do attitude.

REBRAND. Straight away, you must rebrand the mission statement as a vision statement. This implies that you are seeing far into the company's future, perhaps with a slightly mystical aura. In reality, this simple rebranding allows you to be vaguer with your wording. Whereas a mission statement clearly has several key elements that need to be achieved, like a military mission where there are clear boundaries between failure and success, a vision statement conjures a utopian image where there are ideals that perhaps can be achieved, but *at what cost?* Just think of *Logan's Run*, or if you're a bit younger (or simpler) Michael Bay's *The Island*.

This means that if you fail to achieve the objectives set out in the statement, you can still treat it as a brave experiment, like Communism, or Islam.

CORE VALUES/PURPOSE. The use of the word 'core' here is deliberate: your vision statement should reflect your company so thoroughly that if you took a slice of your company, it would be riddled with the values set out in the vision statement. For this reason, you need to make your core values as vague as possible. Perhaps you can focus on 'continual change' or 'ceaseless innovation.'

The purpose of a vision statement should also be to disguise your true core purpose – which is, naturally, to make money at any cost. Perhaps you can add something in about "empowering employees and clients" instead. Also be sure to include some guff about being "an employer of choice" or something and use the word 'integrity' at least twice.

Be aware when writing a mission statement that it is now the law that you include the phrase, "we aim to be the market leader and the first choice in the [personal finance/car detailing/Filipino houseboy supply etc.] industry." Any mission statement which does not include this phrase is illegal so make sure you use it.

USE A FULL RANGE OF LITERARY TECHNIQUES. A good vision statement is not complete without a simile, a metaphor and a rhyme. Try redrafting your current vision statement as a haiku. The more flowery the language you use, the less obvious it is what you are speaking about. Alternatively, why not use a rhetorical question?

Since the end of the Second World War, Britain has undergone profound changes. After centuries of ruling the world, the world started to come home. Modern Britain is now a melting pot, a rich mix of cultures from all over the globe. It's a carnival of multiculturalism, a carnival to which all are welcome.

However, for a busy manager like you, it's a total pain in the arse. You will probably have to manage people who do not look like you and who do not talk like you. But they won't all be Geordies. There will also inevitably be what social workers and other PC lefties call 'ethnic minorities.'

In writing this book, the authors scoured a huge amount of literature on the background and history of the various ethnic minorities in Britain today and the particular challenges they face. This literature is, without doubt, some of the finest writing humankind has produced in the last fifty years.

The thing is, there is so much of this literature, and much of it is really, really complicated, and we are busy people. We were applying for *The Apprentice* at the time. So instead, we took a short-cut. We went straight to stereotypes. And while stereotypes have quite a bad name, there's no denying it, they save an awful lot of time, and let's face it, they're usually right. Here's what you need to know:

Understanding ethnic minorities. Your employees' home lives may be very different to yours. Those of Asian background will probably live in a two bed terrace with five generations of family. They will be in this country illegally and only eat onion bhajis or something. They will most likely be under lots of pressure to get an arranged marriage or not to play football like the girl in *Bend it like Beckham*. They might try to cover this up by saying they don't but it won't be true. You should respect this, but tell them that they are a liar and have brought shame upon their caste.

Black employees will live in a ghetto, even if they live in Tunbridge Wells. They'll find one. They carry weapons and call each other 'blood.' They really like trainers. If you want to get an idea of what their home life is like, we recommend that you watch Martin Lawrence's moving social documentary, *Big Momma's House*. That's pretty much what it's like.

Right, who else? Oh yeah, the Chinese and Japanese are essentially the same thing. They work really hard and are shy. That about covers it.

PC. This stands for Personal Computer.

Are you racist? Many racist managers worry that they might appear to be being racist. Don't worry: just call it ethnocentricism and carry on. It sometimes seems like you can't do your job without some *Guardian*-reading do-gooder telling you it's not PC to ask a black employee if they are wearing gang colours or rip off a woman's burka to see if she's wearing a suicide belt. There is a simple way to assess whether you've crossed the line from ethnocentricism to racism. Simply ask an individual from the ethnic minority you are potentially offending or potentially assaulting! They will be more than happy to speak on behalf of everyone in the community they are from. Be sure to ask them what Asians/Blacks/misc. think about any given subject whenever you can. If they tell you that you are being racist, move on to the next one. Be careful not to ask the same person twice – this can be difficult when they all look the same. If you can find one who tells you it's fine, then it is!

MANAGERS FROM ETHNIC MINORITIES. In researching this book, we tried to find someone from an ethnic minority who is in a management position to ask them to speak on behalf of their particular community, but we couldn't find one anywhere. So if this applies to you, you're on your own.

A good manager will learn how to "respec" black employees.

Taking risks is a vital part of management and for the dynamic manager, risk holds no fear. By following these simple rules, risk can become your friend, not your enemy.

WEIGH UP THE RISKS. All opportunities carry the risk of failure but also the risk of success! Research suggests that a simple visualisation exercise can be very helpful in weighing up risks.

Imagine that you are a pair of old-fashioned scales. Imagine that in your left hand you hold the possible negative outcomes of your decision. These might be losing an important client or being prosecuted for insider dealing. Now ask yourself, what do these things weigh? If they weigh more than five kilos, you may want to put them down on the floor.

Now imagine that in your right hand you are holding a bunch of helium-filled balloons on strings. Ask yourself what colour the balloons are? If they are green, things are looking good. If they are yellow, be cautious. These balloons are the possible benefits of your actions.

Now look at the end of each string. There is a label and each one has something written on it. Read these labels. What do they say? These are the benefits of your decision on risk. Let the balloons go and watch them float up into the sky. Well done! You are now a pair of scales and what's more, you can do a risk assessment.

Just how dangerous is an orange?
Team Risk Assessment gets
cracking on preventing
accidents in the workplace.

DO NOT BE AFRAID TO DELEGATE. Some readers will find the visualisation process described above to be confusing. If this applies to you, do not despair! There is another way to deal with risky decisions.

Some things carry unacceptable risks. In these instances, it might be best to not to do the thing in question. What's better still though, is to do it anyway and delegate all responsibility for the decision onto someone else! This is such a simple technique but works incredibly well. But how is this done?

It's beautifully simple. If a decision looks risky and the visualisation technique above has not clarified things for you, then appoint one of your staff to oversee the project. It's best to pick someone who is overkeen and, if possible, stupid. They will be delighted that you have chosen them!

You may want to give them a cool sounding title like 'project manager' or 'change facilitator.' Explain to them that it is their job to make the decision. Stress that they should make the decision that you want.

If they start to tell you that they think it is the wrong decision and might lead to large scale redundancies, encourage them to look at the issue from a different angle. If they are still resistant, you may decide to threaten them. Be subtle about this. We suggest making off the cuff remarks like "I know people" and "How is your mother?"

Be aware that threatening people in this way is, if you want to be technical about it, against the law and grossly unethical. You should therefore not use phrases like these in an email or in a team meeting.

The beauty of this approach is that it affords you the best of both worlds! If a decision proves to be correct, you can claim the credit. If the decision is the wrong one, then you can blame someone else.

So remember, the golden rule of risk assessment is to make sure that someone else does it.

WARNING: Risk Assessments can be boring.
Do not attempt them yourself!

Health And Safety legislation exists to save lives. Nothing can be more important. (Except maybe making money.) The rigorous training that government Health And Safety legislation provides teaches us to climb ladders correctly and to clean up spillages before accidents can occur. Statistics prove that, prior to the introduction of the Health And Safety At Work Act in 1974, these were the top two causes of death in the office. Even today, they are still Britain's biggest killers in the home, where Health And Safety has no power.

Dealing with Health And Safety can be difficult, as employees believe that spurious rights are protected under this government legislation. Luckily, we have some areas that will help you tame the monster that is Health And Safety:

RESPONSIBILITY. Remember to be less concerned with a person's wellbeing than with the possibility that if anyone receives an injury they could sue you or, worse, the company. If you spot something that is potentially dangerous, it is your responsibility to ensure it is taken care of: you cannot assume that someone else will take care of it. You have to personally take control of the Health And Safety training to ensure that all members of staff are aware of this policy, because then it becomes everyone's responsibility, and therefore no longer yours.

FIRST AID TRAINING. You will need to have first aid trained individuals on the premises at all times. This involves sending employees on a training course where they have to effectively tongue and then hump a plastic doll in front of a room full of strangers. You must use your managerial skills to select the kind of person who is comfortable doing this. Ask around the office until a natural candidate presents themselves.

ACCIDENTS. Despite the government's decree that danger be eliminated from the office, sometimes accidents do occur. If one does happen to occur then firstly, don't panic. If you panic, you will not be thinking clearly enough to distance yourself from the cause. Ensure you have an alibi, or tell someone who doesn't know about the accident yet that "something must really be done about the frayed elevator cable." Secondly, you must assign blame. We've already seen how Health And Safety is everyone's responsibility, and therefore no-one's, so take this opportunity to target anyone you've been seeking to constructively dismiss. Claim that you saw them walk past the puddle, or fiddling around with that socket, or tampering with the lift.

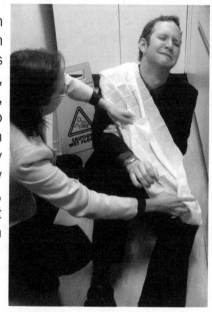

Whilst ideally, a cutting edge, go-getting environment would not have any individuals which hold everyone back, the law insists that the disableds will inevitably be a fact of office life, if you're not able to constructively dismiss them. But do not despair; there are ways in which you can lessen their drain on resources. Any sharp manager like you will know that what must be avoided at all costs is for people to think that you don't really want disabled staff in your office. They can sue and cause all kinds of headaches, and you're busy, you don't have the time! Here's what to do:

NEVER, NEVER, EVER, EVER EVER MENTION THEIR DISABILITY. This is the golden rule. The disability is the elephant in the living room. If someone makes reference to it, even inadvertently, it becomes real. This must be avoided. If someone does mention it, act really embarrassed and pretend you'd never even noticed the wheelchair and really, we're all the same deep down. Perhaps say something like, "I believe the children are our future." If the disabled person mentions their disability directly to you, probably to ask for a special desk or something, then refer them to Human Resources and run. Just run. But not in a way which suggests you do not value their ability to not be able to run.

WATCH YOUR LANGUAGE. Apparently, there are all kinds of words disabled people use to describe themselves. A detailed exploration would be messy, so we will avoid it. At the time of going to press, the authors understand that they prefer to be called 'Super-abled.' Be aware that phrases such as 'spaz,' 'monger,' and 'Joey,' are considered discriminatory in the modern workplace, so think them by all means, just don't say them!

DISABLED IS A SPECTRUM DISEASE. Whilst some disabled people will genuinely make jerky movements and speak strangely, others have all kinds of sneaky disabilities which are not as easily identifiable. The sad truth is that for every Stephen Hawking who is open and honest about his disability, and quite likeable with it, there will be ten people claiming Attention Deficit Hyperactivity Disorder or Repetitive Strain Injury or something. This can be confusing for the modern manager. But do not be afraid. Treat all your staff the same. Treat them all as retards, and you will be fine.

How To Face The Challenge Of I.T.

Computers are the future for businesses, but they can be difficult to manage. They don't respond to conventional management techniques such as shouting, sulking and blackmail. Instead, they need to be caressed into co-operating by a group of antisocial misfits, who need nurturing management themselves. In fact, all kinds of office technology can be temperamental, from photocopiers through to network servers, and this can provide even the most executive of managers with challenges. Luckily, we're here to give you some tips on facing the challenge of IT.

HOW NOT TO MANAGE

DEALING WITH IT PROFESSIONALS. While it's a lazy stereotype to label all IT professionals as nerds with no social skills, *World Of Warcraft* has proved the sad truth that most of them genuinely are lonely geeks. As a result of this, they will seek to lord their silicon knowledge over you like Neo over the Matrix, or Sauron over the one true ring. This can be embarrassing to deal with. When you've tired of them belittling your technical inadequacies, send a woman in. They won't know what to do.

TERMINOLOGY. "What, exactly, is IT?" When people talk about IT, they are usually referring to sex, e.g. "We did it twice last night, and once this morning." This is why anything to do with IT is filled with strange and bizarre terminology: the *hard drive*, a *RAM cache*, *user-controlled joystick*, *groupware interface*, *hardware*... the list goes on. Some can be confusing, so here are two for you – *copy protection* and *surge protector* refer to condoms. Also, *access time* refers to foreplay, but don't worry about that.

E-BUSINESS. They have the internet on computers now, which indicates it is more than just a passing fad. In fact, there may be a real opportunity for business growth online, through what is termed e-business. The 'e' stands for X-TREME. This is business to the max, people. It's faxing while jumping out of a plane. It's conference-calling while potholing in Micronesia. It's agendas tattooed onto bare buttocks. It's the future, and it's here so fast that tomorrow is today and today is yesterday. Technology is moving so quickly that tomorrow may even be yesterday by the time you've read this.

From the smallest company through to the largest, every manager needs to know how to micromanage for success. You must strive to be personally involved in every decision that goes on within the company – otherwise, in what way are you a manager? To micromanage successfully can put great demands on your time and energy, so why not use some of these techniques:

IF YOU WANT SOMETHING DONE PROPERLY... Then do it yourself. It's usually best to assign someone a task, and then allow them just enough time to start before ripping it away from them. You'll do a much better job than them anyway. Alternatively, you could also wait until they ask you a basic question before you snarl at them, "God, do I just have to do everything myself?" Try rolling your eyes and sighing. A tut or two wouldn't go amiss, either. This technique works best in front of large groups.

CREATE AN ENVIRONMENT OF FEAR. Encourage co-workers to micromanage each other, perhaps by allowing them to rat each other out. Create an environment where co-workers are held accountable for the faults of their colleagues. This will encourage conscientious or just plain fearful workers to interfere in the work of others. For tips on creating an environment of fear, use Wikipedia to research McCarthyism, or Chairman Mao.

DON'T LEAVE THEM ALONE. Given the opportunity, your staff will invariably slack. It's up to you to be ever-present as a motivational force. Imagine yourself to be the wavy red line in Word. If a team is working on a project, offer to sit in on some of their developmental meetings. (Chances are they'll be interested in your opinion, too.) Insist that staff submit a written process before the commencement of every task. If all else fails, assume the position just over the micromanaged employee's shoulder. From here, you should be able to observe everything they do. Constantly whisper corrections into their ear. The employee may also benefit from being reminded about the blindingly obvious. (See *How To State The Blindingly Obvious.*)

A business is there to make money, and it's the manager's job to facilitate this. However, sometimes it's hard to increase sales, but there's still a demand on you to increase profits. Luckily, there's another option available to you: saving costs. Here are a few tips to getting the most out of your company.

BE TIGHT. Obviously, you're denying valuable team members pay raises based on the current economic climate, but are you really denying them as much as you could be? Look at the benefits your staff currently enjoy. You will be surprised to realise how spoiled they are.

A good place to start is in slashing the kitchen budget, cutting down on tea and coffee supplies and instructing people to drink tap water instead. (It's better for them anyway.) Put a lock on the stationery cupboard and program user IDs into the photocopiers. You can also put signs in the toilet cubicles instructing colleagues to use no more than two sheets per visit, and stick to your guns on your 'once it's gone, it's gone' toilet paper policy. Make them pay for their uniforms and name tags, even if your organisation doesn't have uniforms or name tags.

Do they really need the lights on? Do they really need carpets, windows, chairs and desks? When dealing with complaints, say something like "You don't have to deal with the budget, Terry." These may seem like small savings but they add up. By implementing these suggestions you could save enough to comfortably pay for your monthly golf day and medieval-themed hog banquet.

CUT CORNERS. This is another management classic to saving costs. Why not cancel expensive training courses for other staff members? If you have a subsidised company canteen, speak with the head chef about decreasing the amount of meat in the portions, or perhaps try watering down the soup. If maintenance needs doing, look the other way. If the matter becomes urgent, don't call a professional – there's bound to be someone in the office with unexplored talents in the fields of sewage plumbing or electrical wiring. Maybe you can use a work experience student, but any idiot will do.

No matter what their actual size, offices can seem very small. The same people work in the same space day after day. Obviously, your staff are entertained when you're there, but when you're not about, they can quickly become bored. It's in an environment like this that rumours and gossip can spread like syphilis. It's up to you to control this environment – you can use this to your advantage by limiting unfriendly gossip (i.e. malicious about you) and by encouraging friendly gossip (i.e. about others.) In fact, starting rumours about people is one of the most powerful techniques in your executive arsenal. Here are some pointers:

THE GOSSIP. A gossip reveals people's darkest secrets so they can appear momentarily interesting, possibly because of low self-confidence due to an absent father. In every office, there is one employee who all gossip either starts with or passes through. It's vital that this person is on your side. Be the "fun-loving" boss and put them at ease with a mixture of flirting and flattery, and then casually steer the conversation towards potentially gossip-heavy subjects. Give away a small secret about yourself – preferably one that you don't mind people knowing, such as your brief affair with Alanis Morissette in the late nineties – and in return you'll be rewarded with a large secret about someone else. The gossip, trying to fill the hole where Daddy didn't love them, won't be able to help themselves. Soon you'll know everything, including what people think of you. They think you're brilliant. As did Alanis.

GET INVOLVED. Water cooler gossip can kill any work environment, as sometimes it can be hurtful or even hateful. There's only one way to control this: get involved. It's better to be inside the tent pissing out than outside pissing in. Sometimes, however, it can be hard for a manager to become part of the gossip grapevine due to the immense amount of respect your team have for you. But don't worry! You can always make stuff up.

ABUSE YOUR POSITION. Don't let a little thing like your position of authority stop you from getting involved in gossip! Remember, your seniority can sometimes help you with gossip. Why not be the first person to reveal a new employee's actual age, sexual orientation or medical history? The term 'confidential' is bandied about a lot these days. What it really means, and lawyers can testify to this, is that it's all on a need-to-know basis. And Little Miss New giving her teenage love-child up for adoption ten years ago is definitely information that people need to know!

The successful manager will meet opposition from all sides. Staff will rise up and demand things like fair pay, recognition, and perhaps even the antidote: but the real danger you will face will be from other managers. Other managers are a strange breed of folk: they are often incompetent, micro-managing simian automatons who are obsessed with buzzwords and have forgotten what common sense and humanity are about. In short, they can bring negative-health into your world. Here's how to get one over on them:

THE EARLY BIRD... Other managers will unfairly seek to put you down in order to make themselves look better, which is petty and childish. In terms of the necessary self-promotion, it is a sound tactic, but there is usually one key element that is beyond them – namely, that you have already started to put them down first. Like a horny, desperate and amoral college student with a hipflask of vodka at a party, you have to be first to the punch, or you will strike out. (Also, see *How To Control Gossip*.)

PRAISING MORONS. Other managers, jealous of your teambuilding and developmental skills, will try to poach your best team members. Obviously, they'll be loyal to you, but you can ensure this by telling other managers how bad your best member of staff is, and then proving it by asking them to look like an idiot in front of the other manager. You can then praise your most awful member of staff to other managers, and then they may try and poach them. This is why it is always morons who are promoted, while those who work hard remain in limbo, unappreciated and possibly even mocked. (This was a policy brought in after you were made a manager.)

GATHERING AN ARMY. As one heck of a smart cookie, you'll be aware that other managers will be playing the same game and making their best employees appear idiotic before you. While this is a cunning ploy, you can see through it. Headhunt these "idiots" to join your own team immediately. Once your team is fully staffed up with go-getting go-getters, it should be simple for you to take over from the other manager. After all, your staff were all once his, so they can already do his job. Be sure to make it clear to your staff that they will have to do both jobs for the same pay. Describe it as an "opportunity."

You'll be recognised as a genius; but if the new group should struggle, the finger should be firmly pointed at their previous manager for failing to train them correctly. This is the point when you can recruit the rest of their team in order to train them correctly, and sure enough, you find yourself at the head of two departments, having staged a bloodless management coup. (See also *How To Secure Further Promotion.*)

Answer the following questions as honestly as you can. Each question asks you whether this is true of you. Award yourself points for the following:

1. Never, 2. Occasionally, 3. Often, 4. Always.

Add up your scores and refer to the guide at the end.

1 I make lists of the tasks I have to do, sorting them by importance and urgency. I then give the list to my PA and go for a round of golf.

2 I recognise the times of day that I work most effectively and therefore come into the office late, take long lunches and leave early.

3 When given a task with a deadline which is unrealistic, I make sure that I prioritise delegating the task to someone else.

4 I realise that while it is necessary to tackle important and urgent tasks, it is equally important to make time to swan about the office slapping people on the back and talking bollocks.

5 As group deadlines approach and the collective stress of my department increases, I arrange as many team meetings as I can in order to stress to my team how important it is that we avoid distractions and get the job done.

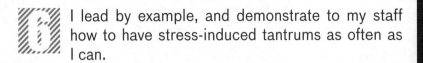 I lead by example, and demonstrate to my staff how to have stress-induced tantrums as often as I can.

I have a watch, a mobile phone, a PDA, a Blackberry, a Filofax and a diary. I place these methodically on every desk I come across to make it clear to others just how busy yet organised I am.

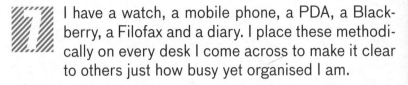 I make time for my hobbies. My hobbies include stressing about work on a Sunday afternoon and phoning my staff at their homes to tell them about it.

I recognise the importance of detail, and am not afraid to focus on minutiae even when my staff find them irrelevant and a waste of time.

As deadlines approach, I find myself reading brilliant management manuals and filling in time management quizzes rather than doing the work that actually needs doing.

SCORES 1-10. You're not getting this at all, are you? You spend too much time worrying about the task in front of you and do not make time for golf.

SCORES 11-20. Oh, just fuck off.

SCORES 21-30. You are heading in the right direction. Your time management skills are strong, but we urge you to read the rest of this book before doing any work.

SCORES 31-40. You are there. You understand that the value of time is grossly over-inflated and why fannying about is a necessary part of the working day. You have nothing more to learn. See you on the 18th green.

ASK YOURSELF...

"ARE MY STAFF
INSPIRED?"

ASK YOURSELF...

"ARE MY STAFF
EMPOWERED?"

STEP THREE:

HOW TO IMPROVE STAFF

ARE MY STAFF INSPIRED?

It's nine a.m. in the morning. Monday. Your staff are arriving for work. Do they look happy to be there? Are they looking tired or hungover?

More importantly, do they look inspired?

It's mid-day on Wednesday. Lunchtime. Do your staff take a break for food? Or do they eat hunched over their desks?

How inspired are they looking now?

It's five-thirty p.m. in the afternoon. Friday. Your staff are beginning to go home. Do they look sad to be leaving? Are some of them planning to stay behind for a bit?

Are they still looking inspired?

ARE MY STAFF EMPOWERED?

If your staff aren't inspired, then your business is doomed. If they're simply running through the motions, perhaps doing the bare minimum to receive their paycheque, then you have a problem. Staff need to be inspired. One way of doing this is by empowering them. It sounds like a lot of hard work. It doesn't have to be. This next chapter details How You Can Improve Staff.

How To Train Staff

"Give a man a fish and he will eat for a day.
Teach him how to fish and he will eat for a lifetime."
- Ancient Chinese Proverb

A company's most valuable resource is, and always will be, its workforce: the people. But, staff are usually complete tools, and like any tool, you'll need to keep them sharp. Regular training sessions are an excellent way to ensure that your workforce is the sharpest light bulb in the draw. Don't worry about having enough subject matter to fill multiple sessions – you can schedule them as haphazardly as possible, perhaps to give the appearance of randomness. This helps prevent malaise creeping in. (If you run out of ideas, you can always run a session on Health And Safety.) Remember that repetition is the key, and to always pitch the level of the talk at the lowest common denominator, and that the key is repetition.

CORPORATE TRAINING. Keeping your staff properly trained is vital to a company's survival, so these sessions aren't about fun – they should be as dispiriting as possible.

Given your natural showmanship and charisma, this can be difficult to achieve. Children are really boring though, so try being as child-like as possible. Ask stupid questions. Be thick. Why not make the material more memorable by using acronyms or catchy titles? One major bookstore once ran a session aimed at motivating increased staff buy-in entitled *The Importance Of Being Earnest*. Wonderful. If an employee has been with the company so long that they are now repeating sessions, this does not excuse them from attending. Why not graduate them to second-year status in your training academy, and have them run the sessions? This frees up your time considerably. Although you can still attend the sessions to butt in when necessary.

INDUCTION TRAINING. "On a blank sheet of paper free from any mark, the freshest and most beautiful characters can be written, the freshest and most beautiful pictures can be painted." (Mao) The first port of call for the training ship is an employee's induction training on their first day with the company. You must treat them like an empty vessel, or – as Mao brilliantly puts it – like a blank sheet of paper, upon which you can create your masterpiece. Treat the new member of staff as if they are a moron and you will soon be able to paint all over them.

REFRESHER TRAINING. Try to avoid using this term, as a 'refresher' training session is not-so-subtle managementese for 'retard' training session. The term 'refresher training' automatically creates a fearless, relaxing environment. Try your hardest to dispel this by making it clear that their jobs are on the line. Only use this when people who have been in the job for a long amount of time are still surprisingly shit at it.

Perhaps the hardest task a modern manager faces is in motivating a workforce to produce better work more efficiently. In theory, no-one should be against this – if the company is successful, it stands to reason that this will benefit the employees themselves, and not just financially. However, in practice, most staff are incompetent, lazy bastards. Luckily, we have a cost-free five step program that will motivate even the most taciturn employee.

1 MOTIVATE YOU FIRST. The company depends entirely on you here. If you personally are not motivated, then the entire company is doomed. Luckily, it's easy to fake. You get paid whether or not you give a shit. Keep smiling and accepting assignments. These can be passed onto colleagues who you feel "need the challenge."

2 GET TO KNOW YOUR EMPLOYEES. Perhaps take them paint-balling. Violence, even simulated, is always an answer. The mixture of strategic, all-out warfare and pleasant picnic reveals a lot about people's true natures. Once you understand what makes your employees tick, you can exploit that to your advantage. If someone is particularly moral, you can play on that. If someone always does what a pretty girl asks, you can play on that. And if someone's a moron, well, you can just exploit that.

3 USE SMARTER GOALS. Perhaps employees aren't motivated because they don't see the point in their work. They cannot see the link between the work that they do and the pay that they receive. Start docking their pay when their work is substandard, or you see them on unauthorised or excessive breaks. Treat sick pay as optional. They may complain, but they'll soon learn the link between work and pay and their motivation will increase.

4 DELEGATE AUTHORITY. If you delegate authority and allow an employee to take control of their own decisions, you will empower them. They feel trusted and will work hard to prove that you were correct to have trusted them. Hey Presto! They're motivated! And it didn't cost you any extra – and they're doing your work for you! Brilliant. Obviously, don't give them any real power and check in on them regularly. Don't want them screwing up. But if they do, then it's their fault alone.

5 REWARD SYSTEM. Make sure you implement a consistent and fair reward system. Perhaps you can let a deserving colleague leave early on a Friday, or move their desk closer to the window. It doesn't matter what carrot you dangle before them: as long as you possess the cold-heartedness necessary to use the carrot as a stick when the time comes. Use the carrot as a stick and beat them with it, and then eat the evidence.

Staff like to feel that their efforts are rewarded by management, but they often feel cheapened when targets are "incentivised" or when the rewards are "monetary." One excellent way around this challenge is to create an employee of the month award, and present it in a company-wide ceremony. Should it be a success, why not increase its frequency? Employee Of The Week? Day? Hour?

Remember, in recognising and rewarding employees' skills, their gender, sexuality and skin colour are more important than their ability to action their job requirements.

Occasionally, a colleague may feel slighted that their work is not rewarded and will question the apparent randomness of your system. You can sidestep the issues raised here by praising the winning employee's "unsung heroics" and "quiet enthusiasm." You can also dismiss the moaner's griping as "sour grapes" and tell them to "buck up their ideas."

You must alternate the employee between male and female, then between white and ethnic, then straight or other. Follow this handy chart to ensure you split your awards equally.

Week 1	Male	White	Straight
Week 2	Female	White	Straight
Week 3	Male	Ethnic	Straight
Week 4	Female	Ethnic	Straight
Week 5	Male	White	Gay or Bi *
Week 6	Female	White	Gay or Bi *
Week 7	Male	Ethnic	Gay or Bi *
Week 8	Female	Ethnic	Gay or Bi *

* Remember that *gay* and *bi* are
just different words for the same thing.

In a hectic workplace, employees can often miss the blindingly obvious. A good manager, as the calm oasis in the centre of the storm, will be quick-witted enough to remind employees of basics that they should never forget. It is important your instructions are given with the maximum amount of earnestness to avoid appearing patronising. Here are a few key basics that should not be forgotten:

EMPLOYEE BEHAVIOUR:
- ★ Employees should gather data before making a decision.
- ★ Employees must communicate with each other.
- ★ Use market research rather than guesswork to assess the needs of customers.

CUSTOMER REQUIREMENTS:
- ★ The business needs to cater to the needs of our customers.
- ★ Marketing needs to target people who will or might buy our product.
- ★ Customers are people who have bought our products and/or services or people who are in the process of buying our products and/or services.
- ★ Potential customers are people who have yet to buy our products and/or services.
- ★ Repeat customers are customers who are returning once more again.

BUSINESS STRATEGY:

- ★ The company should aim to turn a profit.
- ★ Decisions should be made first and then actioned, not the other way round.
- ★ If you have a product or service, try to sell it to customers.
- ★ Plan for the future, not the past. Past events cannot be altered.

The importance of stating the blindingly obvious should be blindingly obvious.

One of the most important objectives for a manager is to facilitate the co-operative efforts of widely differing individuals or groups of employees into a unified whole with a common goal. This can sometimes be tricky to achieve as people can be quite selfish, or they do not want to work for your glorification. Sometimes, they may even go as far as opposing you. Luckily, people can usually be manipulated into doing anything that you want. There are many techniques to achieve this (including fraud, antagonism, brainwashing, sexual favours, blackmail) and we tease out a few of the most powerful for you here:

REVERSE PSYCHOLOGY. This is perhaps one of the most widely-known psychological tricks in the book, so its effectiveness is somewhat diminished. You simply question someone's ability to do their job, and the theory is they are so determined to prove you wrong that they actually excel themselves at it. Be careful not to overcomplicate things by using reverse reverse psychology because you'll get to a point where even you're confused.

FALSE ADMIRATION. This is a wonderful technique as it allows you to flex your acting muscles. You start off by complimenting someone's character or appearance, and then move on to the quality of their work. This means that they are more receptive to your words, so when you ask them to perform a task that they don't want to do, you can dress it up in false praise, e.g. "I know it's an awkward job, but there's no-one else I trust with this. Now, talk to Joe about his personal hygiene."

ABUSE. A management staple. People can be manipulated by abusing them – usually emotionally. The old adage goes that 'sticks and stones may break my bones, but names will never harm me.' This is an invitation for name-calling. Physical abuse can be harder to get away with, so make sure you pick weapons that leave no marks, such as a sock of oranges.

SULKING. This technique is particularly effective if you're a woman. Men are conditionally trained through years of relationships to go to extraordinary lengths to pacify a sulking partner. Use this to your advantage. Try acting snipey, pouting and saying things like "I want you to *want* to do this."

From time to time, you will find that two (or more) of your staff engage in an inter-office romantic relationship. This is only understandable as staff spend in excess of 70% of their time at work and therefore they find it difficult to find the time to meet people outside of the office. (This is what dating experts refer to as 'settling' and often occurs around 30.) Workplace romances can provide the modern manager with some difficulties, but as long as you follow some basic tips you will be fine.

ASSUME THEY ARE HAVING SEX AT WORK. A recent *Cosmo* survey indicates that over 95% of men have admitted to having sex while at work, compared to only 20% of women. This proves that the couple in question will always be trying to shag each other, so do not trust them at work.

Never leave them alone together. If you accidentally walk in on just the two of them, you must say something like "Not interrupting, am I?" and wink suggestively. Similarly, you can destroy any tension with a jovial "Get a room!"

MAKE THEM FEEL UNCOMFORTABLE. Be sure to mention their relationship at inappropriate times, such as during meetings or in performance reviews, in order to make a point of the importance of being professional at work.

TREAT THEM AS ONE PERSON. If you give one of them a piece of information or a task, assume that the other one knows about it, too. Couples like losing their individuality as it makes them feel closer together.

TAKE AN INTEREST. Sit them down together and ask them deep and pointed questions about the future of their relationship. Try saying things like "Where do you see this going?" and "Have you discussed children?" Be sure to ask about various landmarks, such as if they have met the parents yet, and when they first slept together.

COMPLIMENT THEIR PARTNER. Men, in particular, like it when you compliment the sexual appeal of their woman, and you describe the things that you would like to do to them, e.g. "I'd like to pound on that till it squeals," and "Man, I would tear up that asshole. Really mess it up."

Should an office romance not work out, the modern manager is left in a difficult situation. Relationships are tricky things and it is easy for people to allow their emotions to spill over into office hours. As a manager, the important thing to remember is not to be drawn into a debate about who's right and who's wrong. You simply need to side with your sex. If you're a woman, remember that it's all his fault. If you're a man, all you need to know is that she's a bitch. (The exception that proves this rule is if you're trying to score on the rebound.)

SPEAK TO BOTH PARTIES. Malicious gossip is the number one enemy for the manager seeking to deal with the remains of a workplace romance. In order to minimise the amount of water cooler chit-chat, bring both employees into your office – at separate times, naturally – for a chat about What Went Wrong. If they have children together, why not pass judgement on their lack of parenting skills? The employee will be grateful for the lending of an ear or a shoulder upon which to cry and you will have heard both sides of the story. As you alone know the truth of the situation, you can feed this back to the rest of the staff so that there is no malicious gossip.

FACILITATE DÉTENTE. Sometimes, people who have been in a relationship with each other wish to avoid the other at work. This can lead to tension. *Détente* is a French term that means a relaxing, or easing. (From "deux tents", meaning 'two tents', indicating different camps and the tension between the two.) It is your job to facilitate détente, to ensure that these two can work together again. They may not want to be in the same room as each other, but this is nonsense. *Carpe* that *diem*! Put them in the same team at work, or perhaps move their desks closer to each other. If there are any company visits or work trips scheduled, be sure to send these two.

BE HONEST. Now is the time that you can let them know that they weren't really right for each other. Point out the irritating features that their ex had, and comment on their physical appearance. This will not backfire on you should they reconcile.

TRY TO GET BACK TO HOW THINGS WERE. In an effort to gloss over the awkwardness between the two, it's a good idea to remind them how much they used to like each other. Say things like, "Do you remember the time when Tim bought you those flowers at work?" or "You can always remember that great weekend you had in Scotland." Also, it's comforting for them to hear "I thought you made a great couple." Perhaps you can mention another one of their exes, so they feel less singled out. A good thing to say is, "You're really flying through the new guys at work, eh Sarah?"

Smoking is probably the worst thing that a human being can do. It's depraved, immoral and should, of course, be illegal. Inevitably, some of your employees will smoke, and it is your duty to help them stop. Smokers all want to quit but are clinically lacking in willpower. As a manager, you should therefore help them in any way you can. But how is this done?

THE SMOKING ENVIRONMENT. The days where smokers could light up within the workplace are thankfully long gone. However, those garlic-munching Eurocrats in Brussels say that you have a duty to provide a designated place where people can smoke. To help your staff quit, you should make this designated smoking area as unpleasant as possible. It is important that smokers feel belittled and dirty. Locate it as far away from the main building as you can. Be sure that smokers who gather there have an awful view to look at. Suitable views are the car park, refuse bins or local sewage works. A committed manager may go even further

by perhaps urinating in the smoking area or by paying local youths (with secretly "confiscated" cigarettes) to shout obscenities at staff as they use it.

MOTIVATION. Smokers are scum who have no backbone. If they did they would not smoke. (Government research indicates that heavy smoking actually removes  a person's backbone.) What they need from you as a manager is plenty of encouragement. You may wish to shout light-hearted quips at smokers such as, "Do you realise that stunts your growth?" or, "Oh dear, the evil weed!" or, "You are going to lose both legs and die." Smokers will welcome this kind of motivational talk but be aware that they may swear or lunge at you with apparent anger. Do not be alarmed. This is not real anger but actually nicotine withdrawal.

ALLEN CARR. Many ex-smokers have found the books of Allen Carr to have been particularly helpful to them and you may wish to personally give a copy to each of your employees who smoke. This mouthy man was himself once a heavy smoker but successfully quit and built a multi-million pound empire from what he learnt, supplying a range of books, CDs and motivational bathmats. Unfortunately, Allen Carr died in 2006 from a massive overdose of heroin, cocaine, barbiturates and alcohol.

Obesity in Britain is at epidemic proportions. Experts predict that if obesity continues to rise at its current rate then Britain will actually sink within ten years. These selfish bloaters are going to kill us all and it is your duty as a modern manager to fight these pig hounds. Even though you would never knowingly hire a fat person, some obese people are so devious that they will deliberately not be fat to secure employment. Once they have the job they will systematically, sometimes over a number of decades, gradually reveal their obesity. This means that regrettably, from time to time, you will have to manage a fat employee.

WHY ARE FAT PEOPLE BAD FOR YOUR TEAM? Studies show that obese people are much less likely to be promoted than their non-obese counterparts, which scientifically proves that they are bad at their jobs. But it's not just their incompetence that makes the obese challenging for the modern manager. Some apologists for the fat say that they are perfectly able to work as well as any other individual, even the disableds or those from ethnic minorities. But this is not the case. Obese employees display a number of traits which mean they cannot be tolerated. They sweat like pigs. They cough, splutter and wheeze constantly. They leave chocolate stains everywhere. They bring down the entire IT system by dropping chicken drumsticks on their keyboards. They chuckle at nothing. They eat customers. They always seem 'happy.' They suffer heart attacks during work time. Many of them don't seem to care that they are fat.

In addition, obese people are a drain on resources. They are always breaking chairs, toilets, desks and other employees simply by putting their weight on them. They are always off sick due to 'chafing.' While other staff may steal stationery, obese employees will actually eat stationery. Even with all these repugnant traits, the absolute worst thing about fat employees is that they make your business look bad. Imagine leading an important group of clients through your office. Imagine their disgust if they actually see a fat person. They will almost certainly cancel the deal and chuck their guts up all over your carpet.

THE *HOW NOT TO MANAGE* 100% GUARANTEED DEFINITE WAY TO LOSE WEIGHT. After reading the above you are no doubt convinced that fat people should be shot like the wheezing slag dogs that they are. You are right, but Health And Safety says you can't. Luckily, there is a method of losing weight which is absolutely guaranteed to work. Unfortunately, your lardy staff will be too busy gorging themselves on KFC to listen, but try anyway. Pass this technique on. It's incredibly powerful and absolutely 100% guaranteed to result in weight loss. And here it is: EAT LESS. EXERCISE MORE. It really works. But remember it only works if you actually do EAT LESS.

The modern manager faces countless challenges. One of these is the diversity of religious beliefs in your team. Being a manager, we are guessing that you probably describe yourself as 'C of E.' You may have got married in a church because it looked good for the photos but got a bit freaked out when the vicar started banging on about Jesus and sin and all that. Some of your staff, however, might be a bit more into the God thing than you, and the modern manager needs to know how to deal with this. This is all you need to know about managing the religious.

CHRISTIANS. This is the 'C of E' thing. It stands for Church of England and was invented by Henry VIII. It's loads better than any other Christian religion because it's got the word England in it. However, there are many other denominations in the Christian faith and you should be sensitive to this. Catholics and Protestants are the same thing, although Protestants like Celtic and Catholics like Rangers. Or it might be the other way around. Other Christian faiths include the Morons, Jehovah's Witnesses, the Quavers and that lot off of that Harrison Ford film that build houses using ropes.

JEWS. Exactly the same as Christians, pretty much. Except richer. And more persecuted.

MUSLIMS. As everyone knows, all Muslims come from the Muslimshire province of Iraq. Incomprehensibly, Muslims do not drink alcohol. Even more disturbingly, they also want to kill you all until you are dead.

In 2001, Iraqi Muslims hijacked two airliners and flew them into the Twin Towers of the World Trade Centre in New York, interrupting several important management-level meetings and seminars. In 1945, Iraqi Muslims detonated two crude nuclear devices in the Japanese cities of Hiroshima and Nagasaki, killing thousands of managers and singeing countless others. In 2006, an Iraqi Muslim disguised himself as a stingray and assassinated Australia's most celebrated manager, the 'crocodile hunter' Steve Irwin.

These reprehensible acts led to Britain and America invading the Muslim homeland and bravely killing everything, whether they are managers, children or pets. Oddly, this seems to have made Muslims more, rather than less, angry. Some commentators make a link between the foreign policy of America and Britain and this terrorism, but they are wrong. Muslims are driven to such outrages by jealousy. They are jealous of managers like you and the success you enjoy. They are jealous of your lovely suit and your beautiful BMW X5. Above all, they are jealous of the freedom and democracy of the West, which is why New Zealand, Sweden and Canada are always getting attacked.

What you need to be aware of is that any Muslim employee is from Iraq and will want to make terror in your office. They may do this in subtle ways at first, for example by insisting on praying several times a day to the mythical city of Mecca. But how do you deal with this threat? The best approach is to be direct. Ask anyone with a Muslim accent or indeed anyone who looks a bit Muslim when they are planning to do some terror. They may well act offended or even take you to a tribunal for racial harassment. Do not let this dissuade you. If you do not challenge them, then the terrorists have already won.

HINDUS/SIKHS. Thankfully, these two religions merged into one religion in 2003 to make it easier for us in the West to categorise them. This is now a seriously complicated religion. They have all kinds of weird shit like elephants with loads of arms. There is no way to understand this stuff, it's gibberish. To save time, just treat them like Muslims. They look similar to Muslims.

ATHEISTS. The head of the Atheist church is Cardinal Richard Dawkins who, in his best-selling book *The Grandeur Delusion*, explained how clever and great he is and how stupid everyone else is. He also found time to say that God doesn't exist! Don't be daft, of course God exists. All scientists say that bumble bees can't fly but they can. We've seen them do it. Case closed.

There comes a time in every manager's career when he (or she, but let's face it, probably he) will have to give an employee bad news.

This is a sensitive issue and can be difficult: recent government surveys have found that the majority of people *do not like bad news*. There are a few options open to the modern manager.

SELF-SUFFICIENCY. People always feel better when they discover bad news on their own – it tempers the grief with a feeling of achievement. So the first solution is to "accidentally" leave confidential memos lying around where it is likely that the member of staff will read it – for example, on their desk, or by the kettle. You could also try cc'ing them in on an e-mail by "mistake."

HINTING. Subtle hints are often the first clues that most people have that things are not well. The casual use of the past tense is always a winner, so try saying things like 'Do you remember how you used to enjoy working here?' or 'You really loved your wife, didn't you?' Why not be philosophical? Start with "you've always got your health, haven't you?" or perhaps muse "You know what they say – it's better to have loved and lost..."

GIVE GOOD NEWS. Bad news can always be tempered with good news. People have researched whether it's best to start with the good news ("BT are reducing our tariff!") and then the bad news ("And you're fired!") or vice-versa, but haven't really come up with an answer. Why not try both and let us know how you got on?

DELEGATE. Remember that some people like to shoot the messenger, so be careful when giving someone bad news. Then again, this is a great opportunity to take someone on your team down a few pegs. Pick someone you hate. Delegate the messenger duties to them. Sit back and watch the fun.

REMEMBER OUR EARLIER WORK ON DEALING WITH BAD NEWS. As a good-to-great manager, you'll appreciate that an employee will pass through the five stages of dealing with bad news, and it is your job – and your responsibility as a human being – to help them through.

For example, when dealing with a dismissal, we know that their first reaction will be one of DENIAL, so it helps to make the news as undeniable as possible.

Perhaps it would help to empty the contents of their desk into a box ready for them? They will appreciate this small touch.

Then there's ANGER, so it is important that you either break the news to them in front of other people, or maybe via telephone, e-mail or, everyone's favourite, the text message.

Next up is BARGAINING. They'll probably promise to work

harder for less money, at which point you can reveal to them that their salary is so far below industry standards that it's a joke. Ex-employees appreciate this candour, particularly after several years' hard work.

The final two stages of dealing with bad news are DEPRESSION and ACCEPTANCE. Now, you'll be aware that it doesn't matter which order these two stages occur, as long as they both happen. Therefore you can move straight onto acceptance and allow the ex-employee to deal with depression in their own time. If an ex-employee is having trouble reaching the acceptance stage, you can always have security kick them the fuck out.

Employees, it seems, are always after two things: a decent working environment, and more money. It's generally company policy to raise wages once a year in line with inflation, but – like that greedy urchin Oliver – an employee will demand more, perhaps because they've worked really hard or something. Salary negotiations should be handled in an objective and constructive fashion, so it's important that when an employee asks for a raise that you do not laugh out loud. You can laugh at them in your head all you want, but don't let on. Try to put on an expression of pained honesty, and run through the following techniques.

ASK THEM DIFFICULT QUESTIONS. Be ballsy about it and ask them outright "Do you think you deserve that?" Get them to justify their claim, and demand evidence that links the quality or quantity of their work to company profit. Ask them to evidence their long-term goals and accomplishments. If they successfully manage to jump through all your hoops, you can inform them that their current salary is already in line with the other monkeys, and let them know that you'd be happy to lose them, if it came down to it.

BLAME OTHERS. Tell them that if it was up to you, you would happily give them more money. You value them as a co-worker and as a co-person and nothing would delight you more then to see them happier. But those number-crunchers over in HR won't let you, or you can blame "the current economic climate." Say something like

"Unfortunately, the figures for this year just don't allow for increased remuneration." Never, ever tell them that you get a bonus for keeping staff salaries low.

PROMISE THEM SOMETHING. If you want to keep the employee but don't want to give them a raise, you can promise them increased remuneration in the future. Set a 3 or 6 month evaluation period, with an increased workload, and hint that a bonus could result from a successful evaluation period. Perhaps you can dangle the possible carrot of promotion and increased pay before them. Make sweet, cheap, empty promises. If they approach you again at the end of the evaluation period then you may need to make grander, emptier promises. Luckily, you've got a whole bag of them, although it is getting quite full with broken dreams.

Imagine the following scenario. Your team have worked hard to accomplish a goal, with the exception of one co-worker who slacked off. Everyone else generated revenue-initiating ideas, but this one colleague did nothing except claim credit. It makes your team angry. They begin to think 'why should I work so hard to get results when Joe Slacker does nothing and gets paid the same?' Over time, this thought becomes 'I'm fed up with waiting for things to change. I'm resigning.' And, just like that, you've lost a good employee.

You don't need to imagine that scenario: we don't mean to alarm you, *but this threat exists in your company right now*! You must fire Joe Slacker.

Making an employee redundant is one of the hardest things a manager will have to do. If the company is downsizing, then it might even be a friend of yours, or someone you've worked with for years. Alternatively, firing someone is a wonderful way to get rid of dead weight that's been driving you mad, or just a great way to exercise your power and exorcise your frustration. Here's how to handle it:

IT'S NOT YOUR FAULT. The key thing to remember when firing someone is that it's not your fault. If the company is downsizing, then this is in no way due to your management techniques. If the employee isn't performing, then it's not due to your lack of leadership. You'll find that you can't save everyone, and making redundancies doesn't reflect on you as a manager. Remember to continue loving yourself.

FEEL FREE TO GET PERSONAL. Often in downsizing, there's very little to choose between candidates for redundancy in terms of their ability to action their job requirements. In this case, feel free to get personal. Treat the entire dismissal conversation as you would when breaking up with a lover. You may want to attack their personality or their physical appearance – both are fair game. Remember any sarcastic comments or rejected passes that have occurred in your work life together, and feel free to bring them up now. Towards the end, if you think you can say it with a straight face, you can even promise to remain friends.

COVER YOURSELF LEGALLY. The only way an employee can sue you is if your dismissal falls into one of the following categories: unfair, constructive or pregnancy-related dismissal; or sex, disability or race discrimination. Now, you can of course dismiss someone for any of these reasons, but you can't tell them. Luckily, you can bypass all these trifling legal loopholes with the golden reason: dismiss them for the misuse of email/internet. Everyone sends personal emails or visits sites that are against policy. You can sack anyone that way!

ASK YOURSELF...

"DO I HAVE ENOUGH
BANDWIDTH?"

ASK YOURSELF...

"AM I A PRODUCT
EVANGELIST?"

STEP FOUR:

HOW TO SPEAK MANAGE-MENTESE

DO I HAVE ENOUGH BANDWIDTH?

As a manager, you'll be familiar with the concept of 'managementese.' This is the term that your minions have lovingly created to refer to the eloquent way in which you oh-so-clearly communicate to them. Like learning any foreign language, it can be tricky, but there are four key areas you can master; picture language, derogatory terms, Powerful Automated Responses (PARs) and, of course, buzzwords.

AM I A PRODUCT EVANGELIST?

However, unlike learning a foreign language, it is essential that you become an expert at managementese. Let's face it, everyone who's worth talking to speaks English already, and if they don't, you can just talk louder and slower. Not everyone can speak managementese, but it is one of the defining factors of being a successful manager. Remember, the less people that understand it, the more important you'll think you are. It's a win-win situation populated with low-hanging meat.

To be a truly effective managementese speaker you need to use picture language in order to communicate complicated ideas in easy to understand ways.

Try using a few of these in casual conversation, perhaps in the supermarket or petrol station, building up your skill level slowly before you are ready to use them in the office:

ARROWS TO FIRE. As in, "Give me some arrows to fire." This essentially means you require more evidence to persuade someone of your point, but you seem a little bit like Ray Mears or someone like that. If things are getting tense and you're running out of arrows, why not step things up a notch and ask for "a bullet to fire this gun." Every schoolkid knows that gun beats arrow.

BAG OF SNAKES. As in, "This could be a right bag of snakes." The image this creates is of an icky and potentially dangerous situation – almost as if there was *an actual bag of snakes in the office*. Use this to describe a situation you don't fully understand.

BIRDTABLE. As in, "Let's birdtable this discussion later." At a bird table, birds come and go freely and eat their fill, or gather the nuts for winter. The idea is that you will gather a team together who will all pitch in creatively, and because you're describing it in such a naturalistic way, people will think they're in a shady glen in the Scotland as opposed to a windowless office in Grimsby.

GOLDEN GOOSE. As in, "Let's milk this golden goose for all its worth." The golden goose refers to a company's most valuable asset. The term itself refers to Aesop's fable in which a golden goose laid golden eggs, which the simple farmers used to enrich their stock portfolio.

As such, it is a powerful neuro-linguistic programming device which forces people back to their childhood when they first heard the fairy tale. Be wary that this abrupt trip back to childhood can be troublesome for some; if anyone screams 'Please, Daddy, no...' and leaves the room, then let them go. They'll probably leave the company soon, anyway. Use this term when referring to a top-notch idea that you had, or you stole from someone.

KNOCK OUT OF THE GROUND. As in, "When marketing approaches me for ideas, I'm going to knock them out of the ground." This refers to American baseball with the practice of hitting the ball all the way out of the playing area, which is a good thing in terms of the scoring regulations.

This is a particularly brilliant term to use as it links into a sporting idea, showing how much of a sportsperson you are, and it also links into the American business market, showing you to be multicultural as well as multisuccessful. Use this term when you're about to show off.

NORTH OF. As in, "We estimate that customer take-up will be north of eighty percent." This particular euphemisticism has two advantages – firstly, it describes what is in effect a guess, and secondly, it encourages the listener to view you as an intrepid explorer.

PIG IN A PYTHON. As in, "That Chris in graphic design is a real pig in a python." This term refers to a slow moving person or task, but conjures up the hilarious image of a full-sized pig bulging in the stomach of a snake. Use this to pass a negative comment about somebody – it is quite likely that they won't notice as they'll be so busy laughing at the image.

RUN UP THE FLAGPOLE. As in, "Let's run that up the flagpole and see who salutes." Use this to gauge public opinion on a particular issue. The military undertones make this a spectacular winner, as do the patriotic and American resonances. Use this to feel like a military commander.

SLAM-DUNK. As in, "Winning the Anderson case will be a real slam-dunk for us." Be careful that people don't think they're actually playing basketball; otherwise they may turn up to an important meeting in shorts and a t-shirt, dribbling. This is not a good image for the company. The image created by the slam-dunk phrase, however, is so strong that this could happen. Use it when you want to show your physical or mental prowess at achieving a relatively simple task in exuberantly over-the-top fashion.

One of the real benefits of speaking fluent managementese is that it allows you to insult colleagues, but to hide your insults in language so your minions don't understand you. We also include some tips on how to deal with these kinds of people.

BOWLING FOR BATEMAN. As in, "He's really bowling for Bateman." Use this term to refer to someone you suspect is a real psychopath outside of the office. The term is a clever mix between the 2002 movie *Bowling For Columbine*, in which two high-school students shot their classmates, and the eponymous hero from *American Psycho*, Patrick Bateman.

Bowlers can be dangerous to deal with so try paying them off, like in *Fight Club*.

CC JUNKIE. A 'CC junkie' is someone who insists on copying you in on emails that have nothing to do with you. The way to deal with this type of person is to turn on your Out Of Office Auto Reply, instructing them to contact themselves in case of an emergency.

CLOCKSUCKER. This inventive term refers to colleagues who waste all their time at work. Micromanage them out of the company.

MOUSE POTATO. A 'mouse potato' refers to a colleague

who spends all their time surfing the internet or writing personal emails. Speak with IT about putting them on an intranet without full internet access.

MUCUS TROOPER. A 'mucus trooper' is a colleague who insists on coming into work despite suffering from a heavy cold. They infect the rest of the workplace who take time off, and then your office productivity suffers. You can deal with these employees by sending them home. If they refuse to go, you can always hide their chair.

OFFICE PRETTY. The term 'office pretty' refers to colleagues who are only considered attractive when you compare them to other, less attractive office colleagues. This is similar to 'prison pretty.'

The only way to deal with colleagues who are 'office pretty' is to flirt outrageously with them.

PAWNS. This simple term refers not to pornography, but to the ancient game of chess, where the pawns are the meaningless players who are sacrificed early on. This term is particularly apt in times of company downsizing.

SCREEN SUCKER. A screen sucker is someone who cannot go more than three minutes without checking their mobile phone, Blackberry or PDA. These people need the ground rules of meetings re-iterated to them. Why not try treating them like schoolchildren and confiscating the offending item?

STEPFORD WORKER. A 'Stepford worker' is one of those

wonderful people who follow company procedure to the letter, crossing all the 'i's and dotting all the 't's. These people are like gold dust.

THEORY MAN. A theory man is a cerebral person who knows all the latest up-to-date management practices but has not implemented even one of them in the last decade. The term 'man' here is short for 'manager', so as not to confuse the derogatory term 'theory man' with the splendorous term 'manager.'

A PAR is a little management snippet that enables you to limit the amount of time you spend in conversation with your employees. The aim for a PAR is two words; any more than that and you're over PAR, any less and you're under PAR. Unfortunately, being under PAR is very difficult – words like "No" and "Shit!" are about it. Being over PAR is too easy, but if you achieve PAR, then you're doing great. Just think of all the time you can save when you respond to everything with a PAR. Why not use some of the following:

> Get working!
> Forget it...
> Your fault.
> Win win!
> I'm right.
> You're wrong!
> Last chance...
> Shut up!
> Tough luck.
> Enough said...
> Good luck!
> You idiot!
> Fat chance!
> You're fired.

And, very occasionally, you can use:

> Well done!

A buzzword serves two vital purposes. Firstly, a good buzzword covers a gap in knowledge and can be used instead of taking a breath. Secondly, it makes you seem more intelligent. Don't be afraid of overusing a buzzword – it's impossible! Sometimes, you might have been using a buzzword for so long that you've forgotten what it means. Don't worry! Here's our guide to buzzwords:

2.0. As in, "My management style is more akin to Management 2.0." Use this to indicate that you have taken things to a new level. The advantage of saying this is you're using technological jargon which, even though it's out of context, still means you impress people with your computer skills, and your inventive use of language.

360-DEGREE THINKING. As in, "We need to display completely 360-degree thinking on this issue." Use this when you want to see if people have really considered every possible option, but you get added satisfaction from quantifying with a three-digit number.

ACTIONING. As in, "These requirements need actioning immediately." Use this term to ask people to do things – using the word 'action' makes them feel like they are involved in a fun, physical task, as opposed to sitting in front of a computer with a numb ass, moving each hand no more than three inches. They may also think they're James Bond.

AND ALSO IN ADDITION. As in, "These reports need filing. And also in addition, they need filing correctly." Some people may say that you are repeating yourself unnecessarily here, but we say you're not repeating yourself enough. Staff like it when clear instructions are repeated repeatedly to them; it's the only way they'll learn.

BANDWIDTH. As in, "We need more bandwidth to cope with the demands of this project." What you're essentially saying is that you don't have enough time, money or intelligence to deal with the issue, but because you're referring to these challenges as a lack of bandwidth, people will assume there's a technical problem and won't blame you.

CAPTURING. As in, "We'll only run with this idea if you can capture your colleagues." This term implies that the only way this idea will work is if your employee can physically coerce colleagues to agree with them. Use this to dismiss ideas that aren't yours.

CASCADING. As in, "We need to cascade this down through the hierarchy." Try and picture a tower of champagne glasses, stretching high to the corporate ceiling, with champagne flowing down, filling each glass to overflow so that everyone has more than enough. Now imagine the same thing, but with effluence, and you'll understand the importance of cascading downwards. Use this term to shift blame to your staff.

CHALLENGE. As in, "The failure of this product represents a challenge to the company." Use this term liberally to refer to problems without simple – or any – solutions.

CLOSE OF PLAY. As in, "I'll need those figures by close of play Thursday." Use this to inject a little bit of sports-related imagery into setting deadlines.

DRILL DOWN. As in, "We need to drill down to our core competencies." What you're trying to say is that you want to get back to basics, but you don't want to sound like New Labour, you want to sound more like you're in *Armageddon*.

The same is true with the concept of 'taking one for the team' – it's no longer throwing yourself on the grenade, but 'doing a Bruce Willis.' Use this to sound manly. If anyone asks you about a gimp, explain that you mean Bruce Willis in *Armageddon*, not *Pulp Fiction*.

FORWARD PLANNING. As in, "We need to be forward planning with this." People are foolish and will often try to plan retroactively. It's your job to remind them to plan in advance of events occurring.

FROM THE GET-GO. As in, "We need to be savaging this baby from the get-go." This simple phrase means 'from the start.' If you use this correctly, you'll generate a faint air of quaint 1950s nostalgic appeal that indicates you are a management stalwart who remembers a time when men were men, political correctness meant ticking the right box, and you were free to call a spade a spade, but only if you owned him.

GET ALL MY DUCKS IN A ROW. As in, "I'm going to need to get all my ducks in a row on this one." This beautiful phrase means that you want all the pertinent data to hand, or you want everything to run smoothly, but conjures the wonderfully Disneyesque image of cute little ducks lined up. People like this image as ducklings are fluffy, but remember that they're lining up to be shot. Don't name your ducks or get too attached to them, just make sure you have enough arrows to fire.

GOING FORWARD. As in, "Going forward, we need to make sure this never happens again." Use this term to eradicate all reference to the past. Once you utter the phrase 'going forward', it means any mistakes you've made in the past are erased. It's a useful pointer to make people aware that you're about to announce your decision and it's a brilliant way to bring a discussion to a close.

You can even expand this, telling people that you must 'go forward together', indicating that you're all moving towards the same goal. You may even want to hold hands.

GRANULITY. As in, "Let's get down to the granularity." Use this term to refer to the minor details. It's best to use this when a project is still in its infancy. You'll usually find that people are unable to answer your questions in any great detail at this stage, but they'll appreciate how anal you're being.

HIGH ALTITUDE VIEW. As in, "We need to look at the high-altitude view on this one." Essentially, you're asking people to look at the big picture, but what you're also doing is getting people to relax, like they were floating on a cloud, imagining all the tiny details happening so far below them

– waterfalls cascading into lakes, rainbows smiling across cities, projects running wildly over budget – and smiling serenely at all the beauty. Use this term to justify every decision that's questioned.

IDEA SHOWERS. As in, "We need an idea shower on how to fix the bugs in this software." This used to be called a brainstorm until those selfish epileptics ruined it. Now we have to take 'idea showers' instead, but at least we can be distracted by the thought of having light bulbs fall from the sky.

INCENTIVISE. As in, "We're going to incentivise your performance." Use this instead of the words bribe or force. Note also the staple technique of turning nouns into verbs – *incentive* into *incentivise*. This technique can be applied to almost any word and always makes you sound cleverer.

IN MY RADAR. As in, "I've got you in my radar." This term is a subtle way of telling an employee that you're paying special attention to them. You may be warning them about their timekeeping, or dangling potential promotions in front of them, but it doesn't matter to them. They're beginning to think they're in *Top Gun*.

LIVING THE VALUES. As in, "We need to be living the values on this one." This informs your staff that you want them to adhere strictly to company policy regarding specific issues. You may wish to consult your vision statement to ensure the toeing of the company line.

Remember that this never applies to you, however, as you're the renegade loose cannon of the management world. You don't just live the values – you *are* the values.

LOOKING UNDER THE BONNET. As in, "To fully solve this issue, I feel we need to look under the bonnet." Don't be confused with this one: it's not referring to looking under women's hats but instead referring to a car engine. If the car isn't working properly, then you'll need to investigate what's wrong. This is usually done by looking under the bonnet – try sucking your breath in when you do this to indicate the severity of the problem.

This phrase indicates your practical, down-to-earth nature – you can diagnose a fault and then repair it. People will be impressed before you've even done anything. Then call the AA.

LOOP BACK. As in, "Let's loop back here – what are we trying to achieve?" Use this when you've suddenly forgotten where you are and what you're doing.

LOW HANGING FRUIT. As in, "We need some low hanging fruit, and quickly." It's common enough knowledge that as man evolves, he is getting taller. Compared to Victorians, we're almost six inches taller. Tracing evolution back, it stands to reason that back in the Garden of Eden, both Adam and Eve were only three foot tall. The fruit in Eden was low hanging to allow them to harvest it easily, and it's from here that the phrase has come into regular use.

The term refers to implementing ancient, tried-and-tested

techniques in new situations. The phrase "easy meat" means the same thing, as animals would allow themselves to be slaughtered in Eden. When people ask how you're going to deal with a difficult situation, tell them you're after some low hanging fruit. This isn't just a glib phrase: it's a solution. Try repeating it if they still don't get it.

OFFLINE. As in, "Let's touch base about that offline." Use this term as a delaying tactic to distract people. Again, people will be impressed by your grasp of difficult technical terms. Remember to be unavailable for discussion later.

OPEN DOOR. As in, "My door is always open on this issue." Use this to dismiss immediate discussion of the issue at hand. Be aware that some employees may take this phrase literally and assume that they can bother you about every little thing in their life. You may need to invest in a 'Do Not Disturb' sign, or a lock.

PLATFORM ATHEIST. As in, "We need to be platform atheists when dealing with this issue." A platform atheist professes no commitment to one operating system or methodology over another. Use this term when you want to tell someone you don't care how they do it, as long as they just do it.

PRE-PLAN. As in, "We need to pre-plan the Autumn campaign." Planning can be quite difficult; you don't want to just jump straight in there.

Why not pre-plan first? Alternatively, you might not be ready to pre-plan, so you might ask some of your team to pre-prepare for a pre-planning meeting. Being prepared is nine-tenths of the battle; being pre-prepared is the other tenth.

PRODUCT EVANGELIST. As in, "Now we absolutely have to focus on being product evangelists throughout the whole of this sales quarter." A product evangelist is someone who bangs on about how great their product or service is. Use this term to encourage people to talk about work outside of the office as much as possible. You're probably already pretty good at it.

STRATEGIC STAIRCASE. As in, "How does this help us proceed up our strategic staircase?" Use this term to focus employees on your vision statement or strategic endgame. Why not use this in conjunction with reaching the cookie jar?

TLAS. A TLA is a Three Letter Acronym. The purpose of a good TLA is two-fold: firstly, it sounds technical, and secondly, it proves just how valuable your time is as you couldn't possibly say the whole thing. Feel free to use this ATT (All The Time.)

TURN A TANKER AROUND WITH A SPEED BOAT CHANGE. This phrase, to be used at least twice per meeting, refers to generating a vast output with very little input. Use this to inspire your colleagues to put in vast amounts of effort in order to stop the tanker from spilling its oil all over the beautiful, sandy shores.

TWO-COMMA. This term refers to large sums of money – so large, that they need two commas to be written correctly.

Use this to seem nonchalant about dealing with amounts of money more vast than the annual GDP of Zanzibar.

WRONGSIDE. As in, "We don't want to wrongside the demographic." This refers to pissing your clients or customers off. Use this to belittle the importance of whatever horrible mess may accidentally have been created by one of your decisions.

ASK YOURSELF...

"IS MY JOB MY
IDENTITY?"

ASK YOURSELF...

"CAN I SURVIVE IN THE
REAL WORLD?"

FINAL ADVICE:

HOW TO DEAL WITH BEING FIRED

The authors welcome feedback from managers who have employed true Management 2.0 and the techniques we suggest. The feedback that we take notice of is incredibly positive. However, we have noticed a trend in managers who use our techniques. It seems that many of them report that they were fired.

In our view, this is hardly surprising and we see it as incredibly positive. It shows that we have developed an approach to management that is so ahead of its time that many simply cannot comprehend it. Many staff react to being managed in this way with light-hearted and no doubt 'ironic' lawsuits citing all kinds of hilarious reasons, including sexual, racial or homophobic harassment, which we are sure will not come to anything.

Unable to understand that they have visionaries in their midst, companies are firing managers who use our techniques citing all kinds of frivolous complaints such as 'gross misconduct,' 'bullying' and 'flagrant disregard for the law.'

Unfortunately, your bosses may not be operating on the same plane as you, they will be concerned by the value of the brand, human rights and so on whilst you are blazing a trail across the sky of management's tomorrow. Despite your managerial prowess and your dedication at following all the golden advice we've been giving, you've somehow been fired. Perhaps for being mean, or homophobic, or racist, or just being plain shit at your job.

Whatever.

Being fired means they weren't ready for your ideas. The job wasn't right for you. Besides, it's all someone else's fault anyway. Being 'smartsized' can be horrible, you can suddenly feel like you don't have any friends and the ones you do have have just stabbed you in the back.

Do not let this dismissal worry you. You'll always have *How Not To Manage* here to help. This is how to deal with being fired.

SUE THEM. All companies are afraid of lawsuits. Tell them that you're taking them to court for unfair dismissal. Say you have a dossier full of evidence and you'll see them in court. Perhaps you can find a lawyer, maybe making dramatic monologues in a unisex toilet, to help build your case. You can sue for a wide variety of reasons nowadays – you can claim victimisation, bullying, harassment, you name it. If you need hints, look through some of the lawsuits that have been brought against you in your management career. You can also pretend to be ethnic, a gay or disabled in order to sue for unfair dismissal. And if you are any of those, then it probably was unfair dismissal anyway.

TAKE THEM ALL DOWN WITH YOU. Once you have been informed of your sacking, you should set about wreaking havoc. If your company does not appreciate all you've done for them, then it is fair and appropriate to damage it. If you are aware of any other managers who have ever fiddled expenses or misused the internet, shop them! E-mail your most important clients to tell them that you are going to kill them. If you know of any colleagues who are having affairs, tell their partners!

CREATE A SCENE. Some management guides will advise you deal with the disappointment of being sacked by keeping a stiff upper lip and dealing with the challenge with dignity and grace. Wrong! You are better than this. You should create a huge scene that will embarrass, de-motivate and terrify all who witness it. Scream your head off, weep and throw your arms around. Hold your breath until you pass out. Draw a penis on the whiteboard.

GET OBSESSED. Nothing will show your organisation the error of their ways more than a bitter and tragic campaign of harassment lasting several years. Sit outside the office drinking Special Brew and shouting obscenities. Send them letters written in your own blood. Follow people home and tearfully beg for your job back. Stick with it and good luck!

GET A NEW JOB. You've never been more employable than you are now: you're available and you have a wealth of experience. Use any downtime that you have to study *How Not To Manage* in depth so you're keeping yourself sharp and fighting fit for management. It might shock you to know that people now see dismissal as an asset as it shows initiative. If you apply all the advice in *How Not To Manage*, it won't be long before you have a string of assets peppering your CV.

BECOME A MANAGEMENT CONSULTANT. It might be hard for you to get a real job again. So why not become a management consultant? It's even less work than you were doing before, and you get paid more. After a few years working as a management consultant, you should be able to write your own management guide. It's pretty easy, really, except for a few big words here and there, and even then you don't need to understand them.

Allow me to be the first to thank Daniel Mayhew for being such a delightful co-author on *How Not To Manage*. It's truly an honour to say that I'm sharing the page with such a multi-talented author and multi-successful human being. Co-writing is a harmonious, beautiful, ethereal experience which facilitates the birth of great art into the world. But, perhaps more importantly, no-one knows who wrote what part, so it's great to have someone to blame for all the bits that aren't funny, and especially the bits that are offensive. Dan's a massive bigot, by the way.

Huge thanks go to Chris Goodier for all the visual and technical stuff, including the two websites www.hownottomanage.com and www.slagoffyourboss.com. Couldn't do any of this stuff without you and I can't give higher praise than that. Your cheque is in the post. Promise.

Thanks also to the *How Not To Manage* photoshoot team – Lyndsey Carter, Paul Costa, Chantal Charles, Jo Goodier, Lorraine Newcombe and GC. You all looked fabulous. But not fabulous enough to use any of your pictures. Sorry. Thanks to Lynz's office (don't know why they don't want to be associated with this book!), Global for the greenscreen and to Matt Stephens for being such an egoless sport about it all.

So, in summary, all the funny bits were written by me, and all the crap and offensive bits are Dan's. I think that's a fair statement. Oh and thanks to you, too. Thanks for reading. Hope you had fun. Now get out there and manage your little heart out.

Adam Kirkman,
November 2008.

In a way it seems a shame to explain this, but it's probably right to. We are aware of arguments that humour can perpetuate discrimination and that satire can amount to 'meta-bigotry.' Some of the things in this book were hard to write and we had to ask ourselves if we knew what we were doing with it. After wrestling with these issues we are satisfied that this book has a moral heart. The targets of this book are prejudice, discrimination, abuse of power and the idiocy of management manuals and big business. We believe that satirising these things is more powerful than sermonising about them. That's all.

Daniel Mayhew,
November 2008.

PLEASE VISIT OUR WEBSITE:

WWW.
HOW
NOT
TO
MANAGE
.COM

PLEASE VISIT OUR WEBSITE:

WWW. SLAG OFF YOUR BOSS .COM